BALLROOM DANCING

The Ballroom Dancing sections of this book were prepared by Miss Phyllis Haylor on behalf of the Ballroom Branch Committee of the ISTD. The Latin sections were prepared by Mrs Peggy Spencer and Miss Gwenethe Walshe on behalf of the Latin American Committee of the ISTD.

As a young girl, Phyllis Haylor rose to fame as a World Champion and subsequently devoted a lifetime to the art of Ballroom Dancing. The founder of one of London's most successful schools of dancing, she continued to work as a teacher, adjudicator, lecturer and author until her death in 1981.

Peggy Spencer is an exponent of both Latin and Ballroom dancing who, together with her husband Frank Spencer, has danced, judged and taught all over the world. Although best known for their television Championship Formation teams, they are both well known as teachers and train thousands of beginners and medallists every year.

Gwenethe Walshe is a distinguished teacher of dancing who specialises in Latin American. She has lectured and demonstrated all over the world, and made many television appearances. She also introduced to the UK such popular dances as the Twist and the Merengue.

TEACH YOURSELF BOOKS

BALLROOM DANCING

The Imperial Society of
Teachers of Dancing

TEACH YOURSELF BOOKS
Hodder and Stoughton

First published 1977
Reissued as Ballroom Dancing *1983*
Ninth impression 1990

Published in the USA by David McKay Company Inc.,
750 Third Avenue, New York NY 10017

ISBN 0 340 22517 3

Printed and bound in Great Britain for
Hodder and Stoughton Educational,
a division of Hodder and Stoughton Ltd,
Mill Road, Dunton Green, Sevenoaks, Kent,
by Richard Clay Ltd, Bungay, Suffolk

CONTENTS

FOREWORD

William Cobbett said 'Dancing is at once rational and healthful. It is the natural amusement of young people and such it has been from the days of Moses'. Our only quarrel with this statement is the reference to 'young people', since the recreation of dancing provides pleasure and enjoyment, with relaxation and an improved social life, to people of all ages and all backgrounds. It is an ideal path to health through gentle exercise in these days of tension, stress and sedentary work and pleasures. Those who foresake the television screen to go dancing reap great mental and physical rewards.

It is to help everyone to enjoy these benefits that this book has been written on behalf of the Imperial Society of Teachers of Dancing, the world's leading Society, which through its eleven branches represents every aspect of the great Art of the Dance. The Ballroom Branch founded in 1924 developed and perfected what is known as the 'English Style'* of ballroom dancing which has become established throughout the world and especially in Australia, South Africa and Europe. In recent years the style has also been taken up extensively in Japan and the USA. Because of the worldwide spread of interest in this style of dancing, it is often now referred to as the 'International Style'.

The object has been to provide a book for the absolute beginner who wishes to dance socially and gain pleasure by knowing all the many rhythms and types of social dance which are used throughout the world while not being overburdened with too advanced a description of any one of them. The beginner will benefit even more if he uses the book in conjunction with classes at his local school of ballroom dancing. Almost every school arranges beginners' classes, where many of the rhythms covered in this book are taught in easy stages with an excellent opportunity to practise to the latest records. All teachers put the beginner at his ease and show him that to learn dancing is fun and that everyone can soon enjoy it. In the UK the ISTD at Euston Hall, Birkenhead Street, London WC1H 8BE will advise generally and send the address of a local school of dancing to anyone who enquires. The addresses of linked overseas societies are listed at the back of the book.

Of course many thousands of people who begin as social dancers become keen to improve their standard, since in its advanced form ballroom dancing becomes a highly skilled and almost an athletic pastime. For the more skilled dancer, schools arrange medal classes at Bronze, Silver, Gold and higher levels in preparation for the amateur medal tests arranged by the ISTD. Similarly many dancers become keen to participate in the competitions that are arranged throughout the world and which cater for a wide range of dancing ability from the complete novice to the National Champion.

My final word is that dancing at any level of ability improves your health, enhances your social life and adds to your enjoyment of leisure, and the eminent teachers who wrote this book have many years of experience in teaching beginners to dance from which they hope you will benefit.

Victor Silvester
formerly President, ISTD

**Editor's Note:*
English Style—Waltz, Foxtrot, Tango and Quickstep
In essence this was the dancing developed to American ragtime music and based on natural movement (walking steps) instead of Ballet as in the Old Time Waltz and Polka (on the toes with the feet turned out). The four dances evolved from a collaboration

between the best ballroom dancers of the early Twenties in England. Five leading dancers—Josephine Bradley, Eve Tynegate-Smith, Muriel Simmons, Lisle Humphries and Victor Silvester were brought together by the Imperial Society in 1924 to form the original committee of the Ballroom Branch and to perfect, analyse, and standardise the dances and subsequently to examine intending teachers in the technique which the Committee established.

INTRODUCTION

This book is intended for the absolute beginner, whose interest has been aroused in dancing and who would like to tackle the job more intelligently than simply learning a series of mechanical motions that enable him, or her, to 'get round the floor'. The dances covered come into three categories: traditional ballroom dances, such as the Waltz; Latin-American dances, such as the Rumba; and social and solo dances particularly suitable for a disco. No book can substitute for a good teacher but, where a teacher is not at hand, there is no reason why reasonable proficiency in the dances should not be attained by studying this book, provided that sufficient practice is put in to enable the steps and figures to be performed without conscious thinking. If, as is desirable, a dancing school is being attended, the book can act as an *aide-mémoire* of the teacher's instructions and make home practice easier. At a school, having made progress and developed an enthusiasm for the dances, the beginner may become keen to enter for one, or more, of the Society's 'Popular Dance Tests', which are not difficult and are great fun. They serve as an encouragement to go further because they mark progress in a tangible manner. The requirements for these tests are covered in this book.

1 *HOW THIS BOOK IS ARRANGED*

There is no specific order in which the dances should be performed or learnt. This is purely a matter of the personal inclination of the dancer. For example, in a relaxed and quiet mood you might dance the Rumba and the Social Foxtrot, or in a lighter mood the Quickstep and Jive.

2 *HOW TO USE THIS BOOK*

The important principle is to resist the temptation to try too much at one time. Many beginners, in sheer enthusiasm, want to learn every possible variation before they are able to dance the basic movements, smoothly and without effort, and with a true feeling for the music.

The best method is to select three dances—for example, the Social Foxtrot, Waltz and Cha Cha Cha, and master thoroughly the foot placements, the leg action, and the body and arm positions in the basic movement for each dance. Concentrate on the first figure or exercise described in the book for the particular dance, put on a suitable record and practise until you feel that what you are doing is expressing the rhythm and meaning of the music. Restrict yourself to three dances until you can do up to four figures in each without conscious effort; then go on to another dance if you feel so inclined but, once again, start by becoming completely at ease with the basic movement.

1 *DRESSING FOR DANCING*

This is a difficult question, with no single or specific answer. Like so many other social activities, it is important that the dress, whether of man or lady, should conform. What you wear will depend on the company and the place in which the dance, or function, is held. One of the main attractions of the dances which are described in the book is the width of their field of practice; in other words, they may be danced at a small and informal club 'hop', or at a State Ball. You would not go into a jazz club wearing white tie and tails and, similarly, you would not appear at the International Ballroom Championships wearing jeans.

When attending group classes, practice dances, or private lessons at a Dancing School or Studio, the generally accepted wear for men is a lounge suit. In hot weather, jackets are removed but most teachers prefer a tie rather than an open-neck shirt. However, these standards have changed radically in recent times and no one will object to the more casual wear that can be more comfortable than suit, collar and tie.

For girls it is not so difficult to choose the most suitable dress for a particular function, because the fashion of the day will usually decide the issue. What is important, however, is that your dress or trouser suit is comfortable to dance in.

If 'dancing out', at hotels, restaurants or clubs, there can be regulations or restrictions which may be imposed by the management. There is no fixed rule and if you cannot find out what is required beforehand, it is best to dress in a way that you know will be acceptable. Shoes, of course, are *the* most important part of a dancer's equipment. They affect your appearance and your comfort; and your comfort affects your enjoyment of dancing. The same rules apply to men and ladies. It is wise to go to considerable trouble to find a shoe, or have one made, that is broad enough, yet gives the support you need. For ladies, 'Court' shoes are most suitable for Ballroom dancing; open sandals with a 2½–3 inch (6–7 cm.) heel are usually best for Latin American. Whatever shoes you have, it is very important that the soles are light and *flexible*. Your feet, especially in dances such as the Rumba, have to *feel* the floor, to the extent that you virtually press the movement into the boards. It is also possible to buy shoes with non-slip soles, or you can stick on an oversole of soft chamois leather which has the same effect. But remember that the foot should be able to slide over the floor with a reasonable amount of freedom, so a completely non-slip sole will make dancing difficult.

For men, patent or glace kid shoes are no longer as popular as they were: well-polished box calf or suede always looks smart, and is comfortable.

Most dancing venues like to protect their dance floors from outdoor shoes and expect you to wear shoes specially made for dancing. These are easily obtainable and will help you to improve your balance and control.

Never wear new shoes for dancing as they will almost certainly result in blisters; try them out at home first.

4 *AT THE DANCE*

Remember that, no matter how good a dancer you are, it is bad taste to show off your steps regardless of others on the floor, and to impose them on your partner if she/he is not of the same standard. In fact, if you have not danced together before, it is advisable to keep to social dancing especially when in a crowded restaurant or club.

5 *MUSIC*

You will probably start by buying your own records to dance to. If you are a beginner, it is wise to obtain records made and published with the approval of the Official Board, and other dancing authorities, as these will have reliable tempos and the appropriate accenting of beats, *etc.*

To begin with, use recordings by well-known dance orchestras *e.g.* Joe Loss, Ray McVay, Victor Silvester, Phil Tate, Billy Ternent and Sydney Thompson (all UK); also orchestras such as Hugo Strasser and Max Gregor (Germany) and those recorded by Telemark Recordings (USA). But become more adventurous—dancing is enjoyed to all types of music and the current hit parade will always contain recordings which are fun to dance to.

The sound you get can only be as good as that on the record at the time you play it, so it is important to look after your records. Take care to keep dust away and avoid touching the playing surfaces. Keep all LPs upright, in their covers, and stored together with slight pressure to stop warping.

The pick-up arm and the cartridge, with its diamond or sapphire stylus, must be carefully chosen and matched to the turntable you use. Be particularly careful with the stylus, as a faulty stylus will ruin your records.

HOW TO STUDY DANCES AND INDIVIDUAL FIGURES

First select the dance you wish to concentrate on and obtain a suitable record for it. Study very carefully the directions at the beginning of each dance where it is usually indicated that a basic movement or repetitive exercise is recommended to get the feeling of the basic step or action. This is because the dance will be developed from that basic step or action and it is essential to practise that first. When studying the figures in each dance, look carefully for turns or changes of body position with partner, particularly in the Latin dances; often the change of position with partner is the attractive variation of the basic theme. For instance, the New York in the Cha Cha Cha is in side-by-side position, not facing position. The time steps in the Cha Cha Cha are in Solo position. The Fallaway Rock in the Jive commences in Fallaway position, so it is essential to understand these changes of body position to produce the correct effect of the figure being danced.

Foot positions alone do not make the figure complete; the rhythm, the correct position in relation to the room, and the body position in relation to partner are all important parts of the figure. Very often the term SMALL STEPS is used. Take careful note of this, because a large step will cause bad balance and ugly leg lines and could be responsible for making the dancer out of time with the music. In any case, small steps for social dancing are a must. Popular ballrooms, clubs and dancing classes are usually quite crowded. Although you may learn to dance in an empty room with a teacher or a partner, keep in mind that your dancing must eventually take place on a crowded floor and so attention to direction, leading and consideration for others on the floor are essential ingredients to a happy evening of dancing.

The commencing and finishing positions given in each figure are given as a guide to assist the beginner. Eventually the figures must be adjusted to the amount of space available and the conditions in which the dancers find themselves. Try to study the musical value of each step (given under the heading TIMING, throughout the book) and the difference between a slow step and a quick. Dancing would not be such a joy if every step had the same beat value, and the challenge comes in understanding how to amalgamate the slows and quicks, and even (as in Jive and Cha Cha Cha) the faster type of chasse movement.

Good dancing relies considerably on the co-ordination of feet, body and arms, which takes a little time, so do not get impatient. Practice makes perfect.

ABBREVIATIONS USED

L	Left
R	Right
LF	Left Foot
RF	Right Foot
LOD	Line of Dance
Q	Quick
S	Slow
&	*and* (denotes ½ beat)
a	*a* (denotes ¼ beat)

LINE OF DANCE

The line of dance represents an imaginary line drawn anti-clockwise round the Ballroom floor. The dancer who has driven on the right will recognise that this line of direction is on exactly the same principle; *i.e.* the outer wall of the Ballroom is the equivalent of the pavement and buildings on his *right*. To facilitate travelling round the Ballroom without collision it is necessary to try to keep progression anti-clockwise, wall on right, centre on left. For example,

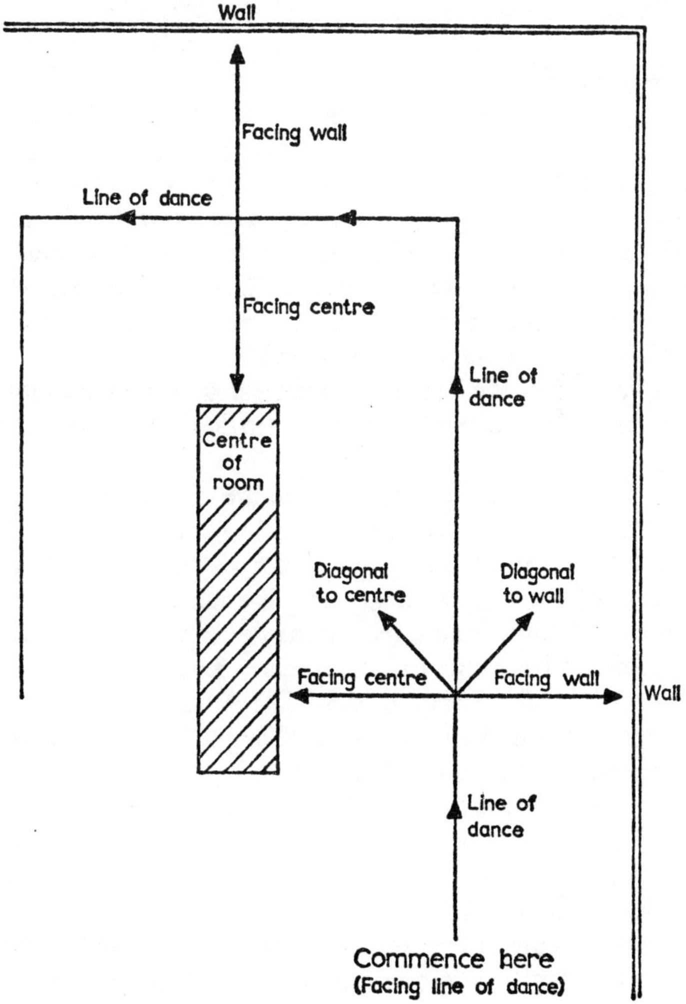
Wall
Facing wall
Line of dance
Facing centre
Line of dance
Centre of room
Diagonal to centre
Diagonal to wall
Facing centre
Facing wall
Wall
Line of dance
Commence here
(Facing line of dance)

if the dancer travels across the Ballroom he will inevitably collide with those on the 'other side of the road'. This Line of Dance is individual to each couple (*see Fig. p.* 7).

ALIGNMENTS

Having understood the term LOD it can be seen that, if the dancer turns a quarter of a circle to the right from his LOD he will find himself *facing squarely to the outer wall of the Ballroom* an alignment known as *Facing Wall* (*FW*). If he turns less, *i.e.* an eighth of a circle, he will be facing diagonally to wall (DW). The same technique applies to Left or Reverse Turns from facing LOD: after the dancer turns a quarter circle to the left he will find himself facing squarely to the centre of the Ballroom; if he turns less, *i.e.* an eighth of a circle to the left he will be facing diagonally centre (DC).

The line of dance only applies to the travelling dances—Waltz, Social Foxtrot, Tango, Social Quickstep, Quickstep, Quick Waltz, Samba and Paso Doble. But don't be misled—most floors are crowded and travel is and should be limited. In the remaining dances there need be no progression round the room and alignments which relate to wall and centre of the room need not apply. However, in the descriptions of non-travelling dances it has been thought helpful to include commencing and guiding alignments.

Where only one alignment is given, this relates to the man.

AMALGAMATIONS

The figures given for each dance can be combined in different ways to give variation. Suitable figure combinations are suggested in the amalgamations section at the end of each dance.

HOW TO INTERPRET FOOT POSITIONS

The positioning of one foot is given in relation to the other, where there are no other instructions.

RF forward: forward in relation to LF, weight on RF
RF side: to side in relation to LF, weight on RF
RF diagonally forward: between a forward and side step in relation to LF, weight on RF
LF back: back in relation to RF, weight on LF
LF side: to side in relation to RF, weight on LF
LF diagonally back: between a back and a side step in relation to RF, weight on LF

This system applies in reverse when weight is held on RF. Where the term *without weight but with pressure* is used, this means that the foot is closed very firmly to the other foot but without transferring weight.

ANALYSIS OF HOLDS AND BODY POSITIONS

Ballroom Holds (Figs. 1-6)

Fig. 1 Front view of Man. Right arm round Lady with his right hand just above her waist, and below her left shoulder-blade. His left arm is raised and bent at the elbow. Both elbows should be on a line just above waist level.

Fig. 2 Front view of Lady. Left arm resting lightly on Man's forearm, near his shoulder, her hand grouped with the fingers together. Her right hand is placed in his left hand and her head is looking over his right shoulder.

Fig. 3 Side view of hold without contact, sometimes preferred by the beginner. No change in the general outline but the Man and the Lady will now be standing with feet about 6 in (15 cm) apart in relation to each other. Without body contact it is important for the Man's arms to be especially firm in order to lead and guide the Lady.

Fig. 4 Tango, front view. Man's right arm is further round Lady causing her to stand slightly more to his right side. His left arm is in a more compact position. The weight is held firmly on RF with the right toe level with the left instep. Knees are slightly flexed but firm. Lady's left hand is placed on the Man's back just below his shoulder.

Fig. 5 Promenade Position. Man facing front and travelling sideways. Characteristically a V-shape in which the Lady is turned slightly to her right. Contact is retained on Man's right side and Lady's left side.

Fig. 6 Quickstep. Example of Man's forward step taken outside Lady on her right side. RF immediately in front of LF with the body slightly underturned in order to maintain contact with the Lady.

Latin Holds (Figs. 7-13)

Fig. 7 (Below) Open Facing Position. Facing and away from partner, Man holding Lady's left hand in his right hand, or with Double Hold.

Note: Normal Latin Hold or Closed Facing Position. Facing partner, slightly apart, with hold as shown in *Fig. 3* or with no hold or Double Hold (see *Fig. 9*). A slightly lower arm hold and more relaxed attitude is used for the Jive and Rock.

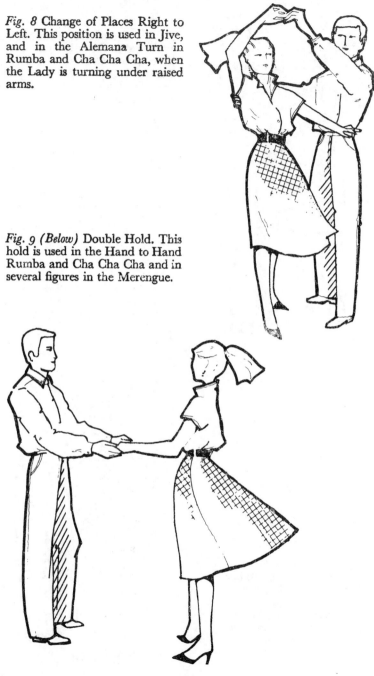

Fig. 8 Change of Places Right to Left. This position is used in Jive, and in the Alemana Turn in Rumba and Cha Cha Cha, when the Lady is turning under raised arms.

Fig. 9 (Below) Double Hold. This hold is used in the Hand to Hand Rumba and Cha Cha Cha and in several figures in the Merengue.

Fig. 10 Promenade Position. As explained in *Fig. 5* but standing a little apart. Counter Promenade Position is also a V-shaped position with Lady on Man's left side maintaining normal hold. These positions are often used in the Latin dances.

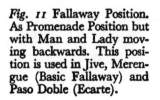

Fig. 11 Fallaway Position. As Promenade Position but with Man and Lady moving backwards. This position is used in Jive, Merengue (Basic Fallaway) and Paso Doble (Ecarte).

Fig. 12 Change of Hands behind Back. This position is used in Jive and Rock etc.

Fig. 13 Left Side-by-Side Position. Lady on Man's left side, both facing the same way. This hold is used in the Cha Cha Cha, Rumba, Mambo, Jive and Rock. *Note:* The positions are reversed for Right Side-by-Side Position, Lady bcing on Man's right side.

I

WALTZ

INTRODUCTION

When the Waltz was introduced into England during the early 19th century it scandalised Society. Never before had the man clasped the lady to him in a facing position with his arm round her waist and rotated round the ballroom in what was almost an embrace; and rarely, if ever, had the dancers appeared to be dancing for their own pleasure as opposed to providing entertainment for admiring onlookers. Add to this the turned out toes derived from classical ballet which were still in use in the Ballrooms of that time and the impact must have been considerable. We hear much of the disapproval voiced by the older generation, but seldom mentioned is the fact that the reigning Queen (Victoria) was a keen and expert ballroom dancer with a special love of the Waltz.

Fortunately, the violent opposition then faded out and the Waltz weathered an exciting and varied career, emerging today in two accepted forms, both reflecting the main characteristics of the dance. These are known respectively as the Modern (or Diagonal) Waltz and the Viennese (or Quick) Waltz.

It would be necessary to study a detailed history of ballroom dancing to follow the various changes that finally brought us the present-day version, but briefly it can be said that just before and during the First World War the waltz went out of fashion in England, and a craze for the new syncopated rhythms brought over from America swept the country.

So although waltz music was still popular the tempo was slower and the steps had no set form. In the early 1920's, attempts were made by the teaching profession to find a uniform basic step that expressed this music, while at the same time following the accepted natural walking action. Finally, it was agreed that the feet should close on the third beat of a bar whether Forward Forward Close, or Forward Side Close. Natural and Reverse Turns alternated by Change Steps were recommended, the man making a whole turn from the position at which he started, sometimes dancing as many as two or three complete Natural and Reverse turns in sequence.

In the World Championships held in London in 1922 Victor Silvester and his partner gave a brilliant presentation of this modern rotary waltz, attracting much public interest in the dance. But it was difficult and gradually a graceful and less demanding version more suitable to the new technique emerged. It was based on exactly the same principle but the man made only a three-quarter turn on each Natural or Reverse figure, creating in that way a diagonal pattern outwards on natural turns and inwards on reverse turns. At the time this idea seemed revolutionary, but as dancing competitions were very popular and titles important, great interest was aroused when a well-known professional couple, the author and her partner, Alex Millar, decided to challenge the other competitors by dancing the new diagonal waltz in an important event against equally famous rivals who conformed to the accepted rotary style.

At a heat of the Star Championships held at Hammersmith Palais in London before a board of distinguished judges, first place was awarded to the new diagonal form of waltz. This was a major development and over the succeeding years the diagonal waltz became more popular and eventually supreme. Thus when in 1927 the Imperial Society's Ballroom Committee (formed in 1924) standardised ballroom dancing they adopted the diagonal waltz which was by then almost universal.

This style became the basis of the dance and, indeed, is

the essence of the waltz as described in this chapter. Over the years exponents have extended and developed the number of figures which are available to the dance but the elegant foundation remains.

THE DANCE

Music. Time-signature 3/4, indicating three beats to a bar of music. Listen to a record with a pronounced melody such as Noel Coward's 'Someday I'll find you' and see if you can tap out the three repetitive beats. The record should be played at approximately 32 bars to the minute.

Balance. This can be defined as the ability of the dancer to maintain an upright and controlled position of the body whether in movement or still. This is especially important when rising on to the toes—as in the Forward and Backward Change steps and Turns. Many factors are involved in achieving good balance but the first point to consider is the positioning of the arms and head, *i.e.* the hold.

Man's Hold. Practise first *without* a partner. Stand with the feet together, toes pointing the same way (not turned out) and the knees straight but not stiff or rigid. Feel the weight of the body to be over the centre of the feet and test this by raising and lowering the heels in quick succession. The arms should be held down each side of the body with the palms facing straight forward. Now raise your arms so that they are at right angles to the body. (You will appear to be stopping two lanes of traffic). Without moving head or shoulders bend your right arm at the elbow so that your right hand is facing slightly above the centre point of your waist. Now bend your left elbow and raise your hand *upwards* to finish in a position about level with your head. Walk about the room in this position and begin to imagine that your right arm is the one that is 'round' your lady and your left hand holding her right hand. (The effect is rather as if the man has created a protective 'frame' round the lady so that he can control the movements they are going to do together, and prevent others from banging into them.)

Hold for the lady. The lady responds to the man's initiative by placing her left arm so that her hand rests comfortably—but *not* heavily—near his shoulder, light pressure in her fingers creating a sense of security but without *weight.* He will hold her right hand in his left, preferably without the palms touching. She should stand very slightly to his right side, and in this position she can keep her head nicely poised and looking over his right shoulder. It is very upsetting to the balance of the partnership if the lady continually moves her head from one position to another—even if conversing!

Having secured a comfortable yet secure 'hold', the task of the lady is now two-fold. She must follow the man's lead at all times—including his mistakes! She must also remember that he is a partner and *not* a porter! In effect she must carry her own weight and in this way learn the art of balance.

Footwork. An important factor in achieving good balance is the correct use of the different parts of the foot. Although it is a fair comparison to liken the action of the feet to that of walking, it must at the same time be realised that in the latter the moving foot is lifted before being placed on the floor. As one of the beauties of this style of dancing lies in its continuity and smoothness of movement, it must be understood that this can only be achieved if some part of the moving foot remains in light contact with the floor throughout.

To clarify this we will describe the footwork of the 'Closed Change', forward and backward, and this method can also be applied to the Natural and Reverse Turns.

RIGHT FOOT CLOSED CHANGE (FORWARD)

Man Start with the feet together, weight on LF. Move the RF forward with pressure on the whole of the front part of the foot. As the foot advances, release the heel of the back foot (this helps to transfer the weight forward). To complete the stride, use the right heel as in a normal walk, taking the weight well over the whole foot.

During this action the heel of the back foot (left) is further released so that the ball of the foot can be drawn up a little towards the RF before moving into a sideways position (*Step 1*).

Now place the LF to the side on the ball of the foot and release the right heel (*Step 2*).

With the sensation of pressing upwards from the ball of the RF and the weight almost entirely over the LF, close RF to LF taking the weight on the RF, feet together on toes of both feet (*Step 3*).

Now lower the right heel in preparation for the next figure.

Lady Stand with feet together, weight on RF. Move LF back with pressure at first on the ball of the foot; as the foot continues to move back it will stretch out to the toe. At the extent of the stride the pressure will be transferred to the ball of the foot and later the front toe released (this takes the weight to a central position) (*Step 1*).

Draw the RF back and at the same time lower the left heel. Then step to the side on the ball of RF, releasing the left heel (*Step 2*).

With the sensation of pressing upwards from the ball of the LF and the weight almost over the RF, close LF to RF taking the weight entirely on the LF as LF closes to RF. Feet together on toes of both feet (*Step 3*).

Now lower left heel in preparation for the next figure.

Note It is understood that at first beginners may wish only to 'Walk' through the pattern of the figures to music, but the more advanced footwork has been given in some detail so that they may later enjoy the genuine spirit of the waltz with its attractive 'rise and fall'. For a better understanding of this it will be necessary—as the pupil progresses—to master the natural knee action, flexing on lowering steps and straightening on rising steps.

Figures Described

1 Right Foot Closed Change	*4 Reverse Turn (Left Turn)*
2 Left Foot Closed Change	*5 Hesitation Change*
3 Natural Turn (Right Turn)	*6 Waltz Quarter Turns*

1 *RIGHT FOOT CLOSED CHANGE*

Precede with Natural Turn

	Man	**Timing**	**Lady**	**Timing**
	Commence facing diagonally centre, weight on LF		Commence backing diagonally centre, weight on RF	
1	RF forward	1	LF back	1
2	LF side	2	RF side	2
3	RF closes to LF	3	LF closes to RF	3

Follow with Reverse Turn

2 *LEFT FOOT CLOSED CHANGE*

Precede with Reverse Turn

	Man	**Timing**	**Lady**	**Timing**
	Commence facing diagonally wall, weight on RF		Commence backing diagonally wall, weight on LF	
1	LF forward	1	RF back	1
2	RF side	2	LF side	2
3	LF closes to RF	3	RF closes to LF	3

Follow with Natural Turn

For the purpose of practice, Closed Changes can be danced in sequence forwards and backwards, commenced facing LOD

3 *NATURAL TURN*

Precede with LF Closed Change

	Man	Timing	Lady	Timing
	Commence facing diagonally wall, weight on LF		Commence backing diagonally wall, weight on RF	
1	RF forward facing diagonally wall, commencing to turn right	1	LF back diagonally wall commencing to turn right	1
2	LF side, continuing turn, backing diagonally centre	2	RF side, continuing turn, right toe pointing down LOD*	2
3	RF closes to LF backing LOD	3	LF closes to RF facing LOD	3
4	LF back, commencing to turn right	1	RF forward, commencing to turn right	1
5	RF to side, right toe pointing diagonally centre, body facing centre	2	LF side, continuing turn, backing centre	2
6	LF closes to RF facing diagonally centre	3	RF closes to LF backing diagonally centre	3

*N.B. In order not to impede the Man's forward movement the Lady should move her right leg back before placing the RF sideways for Step 2.

Follow with RF Closed Change

4 *REVERSE TURN*

Precede with RF Closed Change

	Man	Timing	Lady	Timing
	Commence facing diagonally centre, weight on RF		Commence backing diagonally centre, weight on LF	
1	LF forward facing diagonally centre, commencing to turn left	1	RF back backing diagonally centre, commencing to turn left	1

	Man	Timing	Lady	Timing
2	RF side, continuing turn, backing diagonally wall	2	LF side, toe pointing to LOD continuing to turn left* (body turns a quarter of a turn)	2
3	LF closes to RF, continuing turn, backing LOD	3	RF closes to LF facing LOD	3
4	RF back, commencing to turn left	1	LF forward, commencing to turn left	1
5	LF to side, body facing wall	2	RF side, continuing turn, backing wall	2
6	RF closes to LF facing diagonally wall	3	LF closes to RF continuing turn, backing diagonally wall	3

* N.B. In order not to impede the Man on Step 2 the Lady should move the left leg slightly towards the RF before placing the LF sideways.

Follow with LF Closed Change

5 *HESITATION CHANGE*

Precede with first 3 Steps Natural Turn

	Man	Timing	Lady	Timing
	Commence backing LOD weight on RF		Commence facing LOD weight on LF	
4	LF back, commencing to turn right, backing LOD	1	RF forward commencing to turn right	1
5	Turning on left heel, RF to side, facing diagonally centre	2	LF side, continuing turn, backing diagonally centre	2
6	With weight on RF draw LF slightly towards RF facing diagonally centre. Retain weight on RF (Hesitate)		With weight on LF close RF to LF without changing weight (Hesitate) backing diagonally centre	3

Follow with Reverse Turn

6 *WALTZ QUARTER TURNS*

Precede with LF Closed Change

	Man	Timing	Lady	Timing
	Commence facing diagonally wall, weight on LF		Commence backing diagonally wall, weight on RF	
1	RF forward, commencing to turn right	1	LF back, commencing to turn right	1
2	LF side continuing turn, facing wall	2	RF side, continuing turn	2
3	RF closes to LF continuing turn, backing diagonally centre	3	LF closes to RF, facing diagonally centre	3
4	LF back, backing diagonally centre	1	RF forward, facing diagonally centre	1
5	RF side, backing diagonally centre	2	LF side, facing diagonally centre	2
6	LF closes to RF, backing diagonally centre	3	RF closes to LF, facing diagonally centre	3
7	RF back, commencing to turn left	1	LF forward, commencing to turn left	1
8	LF side, body facing wall	2	RF side, continuing turn, backing wall	2
9	RF closes to LF, facing diagonally wall		LF closes to RF backing diagonally wall	3

Follow with LF Closed Change

AMALGAMATIONS

A LF Closed Change
Waltz Quarter Turns

B LF Closed Change
Natural Turn
RF Closed Change
Reverse Turn

C LF Closed Change
First 3 Steps of Natural Turn
Hesitation Change
Reverse Turn

All the above can be repeated ad lib.

2

SOCIAL FOXTROT (SLOW RHYTHM)

INTRODUCTION

The social foxtrot has evolved from that very subtle and flowing dance, known the world over simply as the Foxtrot. At its best, the Foxtrot is a very individual dance, and perhaps the most characteristic of the original 'English Style', the very casual effect masking a strength of action and a far from casual response to its rhythm. Although the name was not recognised until just after the First World War and the dance not standardised until many years later, the idea behind it had been germinating in America for quite a time, together with a great many other dances created in response to the 'new beat'. It is still not very clear how the 'fox' came into it, but what is clear is that just before the First World War New York was buzzing with excitement over a fantastic dance called 'the Foxtrot'.

In the meteoric rise to fame of the Vernon Castles, Exhibition dancers of outstanding talent and charm, there was no doubt at all that the Foxtrot was the most original and exciting of their various dances. They walked, tripped, skipped and generally moved around the floor in perfect unison, mostly in ballroom hold, and richly deserved the thunderous applause they received.

The élite of the dancing world were soon trying to capture this unusual style of movement and when a very talented American, G. K. Anderson, came over to London, and with Josephine Bradley won many competitions, he set the seal—so to speak—on the style of the foxtrot. Miss Bradley was not only a beautiful dancer with crystal-clear movement, but she had a unique flair for teaching, and there is no doubt that the world fame of the Foxtrot owes much to her brilliance.

However, because of the great popularity which ballroom dancing was enjoying, it was necessary to evolve a form of dance that could express the slow syncopated 4/4 rhythm and yet remain 'on the spot'. This did not mean that the 'travelling' foxtrot was dropped—far from it—but the 'on the spot' dance did provide a means of enjoying the music in a background which large numbers of people could afford and enjoy, and where various bands, big and small, were all producing excellent and individual musicians and experimenting with and perfecting all the new sounds and beats from America.

At first this 'on place' dancing was known appropriately as 'crush', then 'rhythm' dancing. It is now called 'social' and possibly this best conveys its purpose and its limitations.

This may be clearer to understand if approached from the negative point of view: it would be anti-social to attempt to stride round a Ballroom already crowded with dancers, to dance with only one partner when out with a party, or to be so engrossed with the performance of figures that any conversation is taboo—and so on. Moreover, it can create a very good base—should it be desired—for the Foxtrot. (P.H.)

THE DANCE

Music Time signature 4/4, indicating four beats to a bar of music. For descriptive purposes the timing of the steps is given in Slows and Quicks. A Slow represents two beats or '1 2' (or '3 4'); a Quick represents one beat or '1' or '2' or '3' or '4'. Recommended tempo: 32 bars per minute.

Hold This is described fully in the Waltz section, but in very crowded conditions it should be made as compact as is comfortable, somewhat resembling the Tango. In the early phases of learning 'close contact' is not essential, provided that the arms are firm and stylish so as to look pleasant and to lead and follow without difficulty.

Footwork and Balance In this dance it is fair to say that the leg and foot action is the same as in a normal walk, the weight being carried over the forward foot, but not being allowed to drop back when moving backwards.

Unlike the Waltz, where there is an elevation on to the toes on the closing steps, in Social Foxtrot all the side steps, though taken on the ball of the foot, are lowered onto the heel as the feet close.

While it is necessary and correct to learn the figures on a 'walking basis', unless the knees, feet and body react to the music, and particularly the rhythm, obviously the effect and feeling will be rather lifeless and dull. In fact it will *not* be dancing, so although there are many different ways of interpreting rhythm and music there are certain factors that can act as extra guide-lines to the beginner. These will follow the formal descriptions when necessary.

Figures Described

1 *Quarter Turns to Right and Left*
2 *Natural Rock Turn (Natural Pivot Turn)*
3 *Reverse Pivot Turn*
4 *Back Corté*
5 *Side Step (Balance to left and right)*
6 *Promenade Walk and Chasse (Conversation Piece)*

1 *THE QUARTER TURNS*

Steps 1–4: Quarter Turn to Right; Steps 5–8: Quarter Turn to Left

	Man	Timing	Lady	Timing
	Commence facing diagonally wall, weight on RF		Commence backing diagonally wall, weight on LF	
1	LF forward	S	RF back	S
2	RF forward, commencing to turn right	S	LF back, commencing to turn right	S

	Man	Timing	Lady	Timing
3	Continuing turn, LF side facing wall	Q	Continuing turn right, RF side small step, toe pointing diagonally centre	Q
4	Continuing turn very slightly RF closes to LF, backing diagonally centre, weight on RF	Q	Turning body slightly right, LF closes to RF, weight on LF facing diagonally centre	Q
5	LF back	S	RF forward	S
6	RF back, commencing to turn left	S	LF forward, commencing to turn left	S
7	Continuing turn left, LF side small step, toe pointing diagonally wall	Q	Continuing turn left, RF side backing wall	Q
8	Turning body slightly left, RF closes to LF, weight on RF facing diagonally wall	Q	Turning left, close LF to RF weight on LF, backing diagonally wall	Q

2 *THE NATURAL ROCK TURN (NATURAL PIVOT)*

	Man	Timing	Lady	Timing
	Commence backing diagonally centre, weight on RF		Commence facing diagonally centre, weight on LF	
1	LF back small step, very slightly leftwards commencing to turn right	S	RF forward between Man's feet, commencing to turn right	S
2	Take weight forward to RF continuing turn	S	Continuing turn, LF back and very slightly leftwards	S
3	Continuing turn right, LF side	Q	Still turning, RF small step side	Q
4	Still turning, close RF to LF, weight on RF, having turned just over a quarter turn right	Q	Continuing turn, close LF to RF weight on LF, having made just over a quarter turn to right	Q

N.B. The Man may find it useful to know that the above Natural Rock Turn if repeated three times from the alignment given constitutes a complete turn, so that he will end where he began—backing diagonally centre.

At a corner, twice complete is adequate and can be followed by the Quarter Turn to left or the Back Corté down the new LOD.

When learning figures that are danced 'on the spot' or 'in place' it can help beginners to achieve a satisfactory performance if the man marks out the steps by himself before taking a partner. In this way he will notice that although the first step 'LF back' should be *thought* of as 'back', it will tend to be slightly leftwards with the toe turned very slightly *inwards*. This comes about because he has already started to turn his body to the right, which also gives his Lady the necessary lead.

His next step 'RF forward' should remain 'on the spot' but the foot will be replaced turned slightly *rightwards* in order to follow the turn of the body to the right.

The third step 'LF side' should now move up towards the RF before stepping to the side, and as the RF closes to LF there is a slight swivel on the ball of the LF to complete the turn. The whole weight is now on the RF.

By keeping the steps fairly small, the Man will not run the risk of upsetting his balance or that of his Partner, and if all the above is going well he will find that the inside of his right knee will come in light contact with his Partner's on the second step.

The Lady should have no difficulty in following this figure, the continual rotary feeling of the movement acting as a guide to which she can respond.

3 *REVERSE PIVOT TURN*

	Man	Timing	Lady	Timing
	Commence facing diagonally wall, weight on RF		Commence backing diagonally wall, weight on LF	
1	LF forward, commencing to turn left	S	RF back, commencing to turn left	S
2	Transfer weight back to RF continuing to turn left	S	Transfer weight forward to LF continuing to turn left	S
3	Still turning, LF side small step, toe pointing diagonally centre	Q	Still turning, RF to side	Q
4	Turning body slightly left, RF closes to LF, weight on RF, facing diagonally centre	Q	Turning to left, close LF to RF weight on LF, backing diagonally centre	Q

The Reverse Pivot can be repeated four times complete and followed by the Quarter Turn to Right.

The most important point for the Man in this figure is for him *not* to carry his weight too fully over the first step 'LF forward', as this might mislead his Lady into thinking he intends to continue *travelling forward*, instead of which he is in fact going to 'check back' onto his RF. Because of this checking action, the left turn must be deliberate but gentle in action, allowing the weight to be comfortably over second step (RF back) which is replaced almost 'in place' except for a slight inward turn of the foot in order to synchronise with the turning of the body to left.

The third step 'LF side' should first be drawn towards the RF before stepping to the side, the heel of the RF now being released, so as to immediately close to the LF. The weight is now firmly on the RF with the heel lowered.

Once having initiated this continuous turn to left, it is very easy to repeat the figure—say, four times in all—but it is necessary to be *sure* about which figure is to follow, so that the Lady can sense the change in the lead.

4 *THE BACK CORTÉ*

	Man	Timing	Lady	Timing
	Commence backing diagonally centre, weight on RF		Commence facing diagonally centre, weight on LF	
1	LF back	S	RF forward	S
2	RF back	S	LF forward	S
3	LF to side	Q	RF side	Q
4	RF closes to LF, weight on RF, end backing diagonally centre	Q	LF closes to RF, weight on LF, end facing diagonally centre	Q

Follow with Quarter Turn Left

5 *SIDE STEP (BALANCE TO LEFT AND RIGHT)*

	Man	Timing	Lady	Timing
	Dance Quarter Turn to Right, but end facing wall, weight on RF	SS QQ	Dance Quarter Turn to Right, but end facing centre, weight on LF	SS QQ
1	LF side, RF closes towards LF, keeping weight on LF	S	RF side, LF closes towards RF, keeping weight on RF	S
2	Move RF slightly sideways against LOD. LF closes towards RF, keeping weight on RF	S	Move LF slightly sideways against LOD. Close RF towards LF, keeping weight on LF	S
3	LF small step sideways	Q	RF small step sideways	Q
4	RF closes to LF weight on RF	Q	LF closes to RF weight on LF	Q

This figure can be repeated two or three times. To conclude, turn slightly to right on Steps 3 and 4 so as to end backing diagonally centre. Follow with Quarter Turn to Left. This figure travels sideways progressively along LOD, Man's body facing wall, Lady's backing wall.

6 *PROMENADE WALK AND CHASSE (CONVERSATION PIECE)*

Entry to Promenade Walk and Chasse—commence facing diagonally wall, weight on RF

	Man	Timing	Lady	Timing
1	LF forward	S	RF back	S
2	RF forward preparing to lead Lady to Promenade Position	S	LF back commencing to turn right (preparing for Promenade Position)	S
3	LF side in Promenade Position	Q	RF side in Promenade Position facing diagonally centre	Q
4	RF closes to LF in Promenade Position, weight on RF	Q	LF closes to RF in Promenade Position, weight on LF	Q

Promenade Walk and Chasse:

	Man	Timing	Lady	Timing
	Commence facing diagonally wall, weight on RF		Commence facing diagonally centre, weight on LF	
1	LF to side in Promenade Position, along LOD pointing diagonally wall	S	RF side in Promenade Position, along LOD pointing diagonally centre	S
2	RF forward and across LF in Promenade Position	S	LF forward and across RF in Promenade Position	S
3	LF small step to side in Promenade Position	Q	RF small step side in Promenade Position	Q

	Man	Timing	Lady	Timing
4	RF closes to LF in Promenade Position, weight on RF facing diagonally wall	Q	LF closes to RF in Promenade Position, weight on LF	Q

This figure can be repeated two or three times. To conclude: the Man turns slightly to right to end square with Lady, backing diagonally centre. Now follow with Quarter Turn to left.

AMALGAMATIONS

A Quarter Turn right
Quarter Turn left
Quarter Turn right
Three Natural Rock Turns
Quarter Turn left

B Quarter Turn right
Quarter Turn left
Four Reverse Pivot Turns
Quarter Turn right
Back Corté
Quarter Turn left

C Quarter Turn right
Three Natural Rock Turns
Back Corté
Quarter Turn left (end facing wall)
Three side steps (Balance left and right)
Quarter Turn left

3

TANGO

INTRODUCTION

The Tango has been described as romantic, dramatic, exotic, sophisticated, simple and absurd and it may come as a surprise to the beginner that a dance lending itself so readily to exaggeration and often appearing so complicated, should be included as part of his basic repertoire. But it has a long history, with periods of great popularity, and an individuality and fascination which merit its inclusion. The Tango in dance form was created by the Gauchos—those brilliant horsemen who were natives of La Plato Pampas on the east coast of Argentina. The dance rhythm came out of the highly rhythmic and melodious music played to them as they rested in their saloons and taverns. It is characterised by an emphatic 2/4 time-signature and played with an unusual staccato accent on each beat. So great was its popularity that later—just before the First World War—the dance was banned in Argentina. Apparently it had lost its native *simplicity* and become too uninhibited!

The veto was successful and the Tango reappeared in Paris, particularly in restaurants and night clubs. The style was described as 'sinuous' and 'sophisticated' and many admired the 'authentic atmosphere' created by an influx of guitarists and 'native' orchestras. Its popularity soon spread to England and Tango Teas were given where ever it was possible to find the space. The Savoy Hotel was one of the first to introduce these and hired some excellent musicians. Exhibitions were given in the theatres and dance clubs and the teachers of the period arranged their programmes to include this exciting new dance.

With the declaration of war in 1914 however, its popularity waned and it was not until some time later that Tango competitions were occasionally included in important events and presented at theatres.

In 1921 a film entitled 'The Four Horsemen of the Apocalypse' brought the romantic and very photogenic Rudolph Valentino to everyone's notice, especially his dancing of the Tango. In spite of the great impact of his performance, the general public did not feel inspired to imitate him and the dancing profession itself was at this time very involved with the development of all the other rhythms and dances coming from America. Some leading teachers, however, were wise enough to visit Paris and continue their study of the Tango, rightly feeling that the dance should somehow be kept 'alive' in England, and so it was that when the first examinations were organised, it was the 'Parisian' style that was standardised. It certainly had much to offer, being quiet and sophisticated, but it was difficult to teach to the average pupil, and only real enthusiasts took it seriously.

This was the situation in the mid-1930's when a new interpretation was presented by a German competitive couple appearing in London for the first time. By emphasising the staccato effect, speeding up the music and slightly lengthening the stride, the dance took on a new life and everyone agreed that while still retaining its special character, here was a dance that looked stylish and should be possible to teach. This assessment proved to be correct and before long this Tango was being danced by the competitors and taught in the studios.

It must be admitted however, that it took a long time to arrive at a clear analysis of its unusual technique and even now there is not complete agreement about this. The tempo at which the music is played is also a point upon which there is disagreement, but this certainly need not deter the beginner. Different interpretations are a very definite characteristic and perhaps part of the magic of the Tango. (P.H.)

THE DANCE

Music. The time signature of 2/4 indicates 2 beats to one bar of music. For descriptive purposes the timing of the figures is given in 'Slows' and 'Quicks': a 'Slow' represents one beat; and a 'Quick' represents half a beat. '*One and*', or '*Two and*', equals '*Slow*', while '*One*' or '*and*' or '*Two*' or '*and*' equal '*Quick*'. Tempo: approximately 33 bars to the minute.

Hold, Balance and Footwork. Although many different interpretations have appeared, at no time have these deviated from the theme of a partnership in which the man is dominant.

With this idea in mind we can understand the need for a closer hold than in the Waltz; in effect, the man places his right arm further round the lady and—to balance this picture—closes his left forearm slightly inwards (see Fig. 4). This closer hold, apart from creating a more compact appearance, will inevitably bring the lady slightly more to his right side. Another effect of this hold is that when walking forward the right side of the body appears to take the lead and the step taken with the right foot will be a little 'open' in position, with the right foot angled slightly leftwards to the line of travel.

To harmonise with the above the left foot is also angled leftwards in a direct line in front of the supporting right foot—matching the line of the body. A very common fault is to place the left foot *across* the line of the right foot thus overlocking the thighs; this distorts the body line and of course restricts movement.

Lady—Hold and Balance. If the man has taken up the position already described for him, the lady will find that he will hold her right hand a little more closely, with her forearm drawn inwards and facing downwards. Her left arm will now tend to be further round her partner and a little lower than in Waltz or Quickstep. Her left hand can then be placed under his left shoulder blade, with her fingers held together, slight pressure on the thumb and first finger and the palm facing downwards. The head and shoulders should be nicely poised as in other 'contact' dances.

Forward Walk. Stand with the body in the position described in the hold with the feet together. Now slip the right foot a few inches back so that the right toe is level with the left instep; this will help to hold the knees in a slightly flexed but very *firm* position.

With weight on the stationary foot (RF), place the LF forward—first onto the heel, then the whole foot, as in a normal walk. The heel of the back foot (RF) is now released but some pressure is maintained on the ball of the foot which is still in contact with the floor, although the weight of the body is almost entirely over the forward foot. Count '*One and*' or '*Slow*'.

As the weight is transferred fully over the front foot (LF) the back foot moves up with the toe skimming the floor lightly, then as it approaches the forward foot, it will be lifted and placed forward first on the heel, then the whole of the foot. Count '*Two and*' or '*Slow*'.

Backward Walk. In contrast to the Forward Walk, the important point to remember is that the weight must not be taken too quickly over the foot stepping back.

Stand with the body in Tango hold and with feet together. Now slip the left foot forward a few inches so that the left heel is level with the right instep. The knees are now slightly flexed but firm.

With weight on the stationary left foot, place the right foot back on the ball of the foot, then release the toe of the front foot keeping slight pressure on the heel. The weight is now moving towards the back foot (RF). Count '*One and*' or '*Slow*'.

Taking the weight entirely over the back foot (RF) lift the front foot slightly and place it sharply back, releasing the toe of the right foot; the right heel lowers just before the left foot passes, thus making a second walk with the left foot. Count '*Two and*' or '*Slow*'.

The instructions on the Hold, Balance and Footwork may appear complicated, but study them carefully for without doubt they will, if understood, add considerably to the pleasure of performing the dance.

Figures Described The figures have been chosen to fulfil the needs of a beginner attempting this dance for the first time.

1 *Rock Turn*
2 *Basic Reverse Turn*
3 *Open Reverse Turn, partner in line, Closed Finish*
4 *Back Corté*
5 *Walks into Closed Promenade*

1 *ROCK TURN*

	Man	Timing	Lady	Timing
	Commence facing diagonally wall, weight on RF		Commence backing diagonally wall, weight on LF	
	LF forward (One Walk)	S	RF back (One Walk)	S
1	RF forward, commencing to turn right	S	LF back, commencing to turn right	S
2	LF side and slightly back, backing centre	Q	Move RF slightly rightwards between Man's feet, taking weight onto it	Q
3	Transfer weight forward onto RF between Lady's feet	Q	Move LF slightly leftwards, taking weight onto it	Q
4	Very small step back LF	S	RF very small step forward	S
5	RF back to centre, turning slightly left	Q	LF forward to centre, commencing to turn left	Q

	Man	Timing	Lady	Timing
6	LF to side, left toe turned slightly to left, body facing wall	Q	RF side and slightly back continuing turn, backing diagonally wall	Q
7	Turning body to left, RF closes to LF slightly back, weight now on RF	S	Continuing body turn, close LF to RF slightly forward, weight now on LF	S
	End facing diagonally wall		End backing diagonally wall	

N.B. The Beginner can repeat this Walk and Rock Turn continuously round the Ballroom for practice.

2 *BASIC REVERSE TURN*

	Man	Timing	Lady	Timing
	Commence facing diagonally centre, weight on LF		Commence backing diagonally centre, weight on RF	
	RF forward (One Walk)	S	LF back (One Walk)	S
1	LF forward, commencing to turn left	Q	RF back, commencing to turn left	Q
2	Continuing turn, RF side and slightly back, almost backing LOD	Q	Continuing turn, LF back to end in sideways position, toe pointing down LOD	Q
3	Continuing turn, cross LF in front of RF taking weight onto LF backing LOD	S	Continuing turn, RF closes to LF slightly back, weight on RF facing LOD	S
4	RF back, commencing to turn left	Q	LF forward, commencing to turn left	Q
5	Continuing turn, LF sideways, left toe turned slightly to left, body facing wall	Q	Continuing turn, RF side and slightly back, backing diagonally wall	Q
6	Turning body to left, RF closes to LF slightly back, weight now on RF	S	Continuing body turn, close LF to RF slightly forward, weight now on LF	S
	End facing diagonally wall		End backing diagonally wall	

N.B. The Basic Reverse Turn can be danced *without* turning on the last 3 Steps in which case it will finish backing LOD to be followed by the Corté.

3 *OPEN REVERSE TURN CLOSED FINISH*

	Man	Timing	Lady	Timing
	Commence facing diagonally centre, weight on LF, RF forward (One Walk)	S	Commence backing diagonally centre, weight on RF, LF back (One Walk)	S
1	LF forward, commencing to turn left	Q	RF back, commencing to turn left	Q
2	RF side and slightly back, continuing turn backing LOD	Q	Continuing turn, LF closes to RF, LF pointing down LOD releasing right heel	Q
3	LF back, backing LOD	S	RF forward, facing LOD	S
4	RF back, commencing to turn left	Q	LF forward, commencing to turn left	Q
5	Continuing to turn left, LF sideways, left toe pointing slightly leftwards, body facing wall	Q	Continuing turn, RF side and slightly back, backing diagonally wall	Q
6	Turning body to left, RF closes to LF slightly back, weight on RF, facing diagonally wall	S	LF closes to RF slightly forward, weight on LF, backing diagonally wall	S
	Follow with Walk forward on LF		Follow with Walk backward on RF	

4 *THE BACK CORTÉ*

	Man	**Timing**	**Lady**	**Timing**
	Commence with feet together, RF slightly back, backing LOD, weight on RF		Commence with feet together, RF slightly back, weight on LF facing LOD	
1	LF back	S	RF forward	S
2	RF back, commencing to turn left	Q	LF forward, commencing to turn left	Q
3	Continuing to turn left, LF sideways, left toe pointing slightly leftwards, body facing wall	Q	RF side and slightly back, continuing turn, backing diagonally wall	Q
4	Turning body left, RF closes to LF slightly back, weight now on RF. End facing diagonally wall	S	Continuing body turn, close LF to RF slightly forward, weight now on LF. End backing diagonally wall	S
	Follow with Walk on LF		Follow with Walk on RF	

Description of Promenade Position. This picture deviates from the normal situation of the Man travelling forwards and the Lady backwards, and vice versa. In effect the body-line of the couple is V-shaped with only the Man's right side and the Lady's left side in contact (Fig. 5).

5 *WALKS INTO CLOSED PROMENADE POSITION*

Man	**Timing**	**Lady**	**Timing**
Preceded by Forward Walk on LF facing diagonally wall	S	Preceded by Backward Walk on RF backing diagonally wall	S
Commence facing diagonally wall, weight on LF		Commence backing diagonally wall, weight on RF	
RF forward, preparing to lead Lady into Promenade Position	Q	LF back	Q

	Man	Timing	Lady	Timing
	Turning body slightly, right, tap LF to side of RF, small step, keeping weight on RF, at same time leading Lady to turn slightly to her right in Promenade Position	Q	With slight turn to right on LF tap RF to side of LF, small step keeping weight on LF. End in Promenade Position facing diagonally centre	Q
1	LF to side in Promenade Position along LOD, LF pointing diagonally wall	S	RF to side in Promenade Position along LOD, RF pointing diagonally centre	S
2	RF draws towards LF and is then placed forward and across LF in Promenade Position	Q	LF draws towards RF and is then placed forward and across in Promenade Position, commencing to turn body left	Q
3	LF side and slightly forward, leading Lady to turn to left	Q	Continuing to turn, RF side and slightly back, backing diagonally wall	Q
4	Turning body to left, RF closes to LF slightly back, weight now on RF	S	Continuing body turn, close LF to RF slightly forward, weight now on LF	S
	End facing diagonally wall in line with Lady		End backing diagonally wall in line with Man	

AMALGAMATIONS

A One Walk on LF
Rock Turn, repeated continuously round Ballroom (see page 7)

B One Walk on LF
Rock Turn, end facing LOD
Two Walks, LF and RF, towards diagonally centre;
Basic Reverse Turn, end backing LOD (no turn on last 3 Steps)
Back Corté, commence backing LOD, end facing diagonally wall

C Commence facing diagonally wall
Four Walks curving leftwards to end facing diagonally centre LRLR
Open Reverse Turn, Lady in line
Closed Finish
Two Walks to Promenade Position
Closed Promenade
One Walk LF
Rock Turn

4

SOCIAL QUICKSTEP
(Quick Rhythm)

INTRODUCTION

A great many people, especially students, wrongly assume that the 'Social Quickstep' preceded the development of the orthodox Quickstep but, as with the Social Foxtrot, this was not the case and this seems a good opportunity to explain what really happened.

Imagine the period as about the early 1930's when the really enthusiastic dancers had their own favourite, exclusive (and expensive) dance clubs, where they were able to move freely and where so much that is now taken for granted as the 'English Style' originally came into being.

The beginner would visit the few well-known teachers and after private lessons 'graduate' to the Tea Dance or Weekly Evening Dance. There was also much entertaining by important society hostesses in their own Ballrooms where dancing played a very important part, especially for the débutantes.

Against this background the question of 'social' dancing did not arise. 'Ballroom' dancing was enjoyed by a small group and, judging by today's nostalgia for the period, everyone seems to have enjoyed themselves very much indeed.

However, as economic difficulties arose, this background faded out; now it was the turn of the very popular Palais de Danse to take over not only the enthusiasts, but a completely new public who of course needed a new approach. Much effort has been made to 'codify' what this approach should be but only comparatively recently has it been given the attention it deserves; without strenuous effort this simple 'walking' variation of the Quickstep can be adapted to almost any tempo and danced with confidence in any part of the world—Britain or Bangkok! (P.H.)

THE DANCE

Music. Time signature 4/4, indicating four beats to one bar of music. For descriptive purposes the timing of the figure is given in Slows and Quicks: 'Slow' represents two beats—'*One, Two*' or '*Three, Four*'; 'Quick' represents one beat—'*One*' or '*Two*' or '*Three*' or '*Four*'. Tempo recommended is 52 bars per minute.

Hold. As Social Foxtrot.

Balance and Footwork. Basically the same as in Social Foxtrot but, due to the increased speed of the music, the steps will tend to be shorter and the heel-leads less pronounced. There are many different ways of expressing rhythm through the body, knees and feet, but perhaps the most unattractive style is the use of the arms (known as Pump-handling). One rhythmic interpretation which can be introduced is a Charleston action; this is simple to learn, always fashionable and can be applied as the dancer feels inspired.

A description of this and a method of practice are given at the end of this section.

Figures Described

1 *Quarter Turn to Right. Quarter Turn to Left*
2 *Natural Rock Turn (Natural Pivot Turn)*
3 *Reverse Pivot Turn*
4 *Back Corté*
5 *Side Step*

1 *THE QUARTER TURNS*

Steps 1–4: Quarter Turn to Right. Steps 5–8: Quarter Turn to Left

	Man	Timing	Lady	Timing
	Commence facing diagonally wall, weight on RF		Commence backing diagonally wall, weight on LF	
1	LF forward	S	RF back	S
2	RF forward, commencing to turn right	S	LF back, commencing to turn right	S
3	Continuing turn, LF small step to side, facing wall	Q	Still turning, RF side, small step	Q
4	Still turning slightly, RF almost closes to LF, backing diagonally centre, weight on RF	Q	LF almost closes to RF facing diagonally centre, weight on LF	Q
5	LF back	S	RF forward	S
6	RF back, commencing to turn left	S	LF forward, commencing to turn left	S
7	Draw LF back to end with left heel closing to right heel. Toe pointing diagonally wall	Q	Continuing to turn left, RF to side, backing wall	Q
8	Turning body to left, close RF to LF facing diagonally wall, weight on RF	Q	Still turning, LF closes to RF backing diagonally wall, weight on LF	Q

2 *THE NATURAL ROCK TURN (NATURAL PIVOT TURN)*

In this figure the pattern, number of steps and alignment are exactly the same as in the Social Foxtrot (see page 30). On account of the faster music it is not necessary to close the feet completely on the fourth step.

3 *THE REVERSE PIVOT TURN*

For this figure also the number of steps and pattern are the same as in the Social Foxtrot (see page 32).

On account of the speed of the music the action of the

feet on Steps 3 and 4 are identical with Steps 3 and 4 of the Quarter Turn to left.

4 *THE BACK CORTÉ*

	Man	Timing	Lady	Timing
	Preceded by Quarter Turn to right. Commence backing diagonally centre, weight on RF		Preceded by Quarter Turn to right. Commence facing diagonally centre, weight on LF	
1	LF back	S	RF forward	S
2	RF back	S	LF forward	S
3	LF small step to side	Q	RF to side	Q
4	RF almost closes to LF, end backing diagonally centre, weight on RF	Q	LF almost closes to RF, end facing diagonally centre, weight on LF	Q
	Follow with Quarter Turn to left		Follow with Quarter Turn to left	

5 *THE SIDE STEP*

Precede with Quarter Turn to left. Man facing wall, weight on RF

	Man	Timing	Lady	Timing
	Commence facing wall, weight on RF		Commence facing centre, weight on LF	
1	LF to side	S	RF to side	S
2	Close RF to LF	S	LF closes to RF	S
3	LF very small step to side	Q	RF very small step to side	Q
4	Close RF to LF	Q	LF closes to RF	Q

N.B. Dance three times, turning slightly to right between third and fourth steps of third side step. End backing diagonally centre. Follow with Quarter Turn left.

SUGGESTED AMALGAMATIONS

A Quarter Turn to right, Quarter Turn to left, end facing diagonally wall
Quarter Turn to right, end backing diagonally centre
Four Natural Pivot Turns, end backing diagonally centre
Quarter Turn to left, end facing diagonally wall

B Quarter Turn right, Quarter Turn left, end facing wall
Side Step. Dance three times, end backing diagonally centre
Quarter Turn to left

C Quarter Turn right
Back Corté
Quarter Turn to left
Quarter Turn to right
Quarter Turn to left, end facing wall
Three Side Steps, end backing diagonally centre
Quarter Turn to left
Three Reverse Pivot Turns, end facing diagonally wall

THE CHARLESTON LILT

Moving Forward:

Stand with feet together, arms in Ballroom Hold or held easily at sides, weight on RF, facing LOD

1 Step forward onto LF, knee straight, body slightly braced; leave right toe in place behind LF (*Count 1 or Quick*)
Now flex left knee slightly, RF still in place (*Count 2 or Quick*)

2 Step smartly forward onto RF, knee straight, body slightly braced, left toe in place behind RF (*Count 3 or Quick*)
Flex right knee slightly, left toe still in place (*Count 4 or Quick*)

Practise moving forward until it feels quite natural.

Moving Backward:

Stand with feet together, weight on LF, backing LOD

1 Step back onto RF, taking weight over the foot, but keeping front LF in place (*Count 1 or Quick*)

Now flex right knee slightly, keeping LF still in place (*Count 2 or Quick*)

2 Step smartly back onto LF, keeping RF in place, knee straight, body slightly braced (*Count 3 or Quick*)
Flex left knee very slightly, keeping RF in place (*Count 4 or Quick*)

These movements should be practised to music, without a partner at first and preferably at home, moving backwards and forwards until the action feels natural, after which it should be possible to introduce this action into the figures of the dance.

5

QUICKSTEP

INTRODUCTION

The history of this dance is difficult to trace because, unlike most other Ballroom dances that are now universally popular, it was not directly inspired by the sudden emergence of a new 'beat' or rhythm or of a particular kind of music coming from abroad, nor were there any stage or screen personalities exhibiting it when it was first evolved.

By about 1926 the farmyard collection—Bunny-Hug, Turkey Trot and others—had all lost favour, leaving the Foxtrot, Waltz, Tango and One-step (originally invented by the Vernon Castles, but to different music), as the required dances for entry to championships.

It is with this One-step that we are concerned, because there is no doubt that it instilled in the dancers of that period certain qualities which were to become an integral part of the 'English Style' in general, and of the Quickstep at certain times in its career. Two of these essential qualities were that the man's forward and backward steps must be in 'straight alignment' with the lady's together with a continuity of progression created by a firm swing of the leg from the hip while gliding lightly round the floor in the manner of a walk (*i.e.* heel-leading). Lively and smart when well done to the rather martial type of music (Valencia was a firm favourite), it can be seen that these essentials were good training for the future.

At this time great changes were taking place in dance bands and dance music; new and more exciting tunes were being produced, young people had the opportunity to improvise and practise at home to records and the 'Big Bands' in the hands of famous leaders were providing

Jazz and Beat music which had great popular appeal.

So it was that the music of the One-step with its lack of syncopation gradually faded out; the music died and the dance died with it. The bands with the help of radio literally 'called the tune' and the dancers had to follow, thus creating for themselves a new interpretation of Foxtrot to suit music now played very much faster.

Then came the Charleston explosion. An off-beat dance of quite extraordinary vitality, the Charleston combines a flexing and stretching of the knees with an in-and-out twisting of the feet and a contra swing of the arms, if danced without a partner. It is extremely exciting to do and to watch. Ballroom floors everywhere became a flailing mass of arms and legs, but not for long. PCQ ('Please Charleston Quietly') and 'No Kicking Please' boards were soon produced and rules strictly enforced, and so the Charleston faded and died, although it left a very vivid impression on the young and gifted dancers of the day.

The 'Star' Championship (promoted by the newspaper of that name) had already in 1927 replaced the One-step with the 'Quick-time Foxtrot and Charleston'. Following upon this the Imperial Society, with 'The Dancing Times' decided to organise the British Professional Championship and also to eliminate the One-step, and replace it with 'The Quickstep' (thus getting rid of a descriptive, but very cumbersome name).

The overall Championship was taken by Maxwell Stewart and Pat Sykes, but the Quickstep section was won by Alec Millar and Phyllis Haylor, who without a vestige of kicking had managed to convey the charm of the Charleston, together with other very simple little figures including the Millar Cross (now called Cross Swivel) all fitting easily into the 'new' music. This competition put the Quickstep firmly on the map, and it has been one of the standard four English Style dances ever since. (P.H.)

THE DANCE

Various important points must be mastered to help to produce an enjoyable performance of the Quickstep, as distinct from the Social Quickstep.

Contact with Partner. As this is really the corner-stone or the beauty of the original 'English style', expressed ideally as 'two people moving as one', it is vital to grasp that this effect can only be arrived at if it is clear that one or other of the partnership is moving either on the 'outside' or the 'inside' of parts of a circle that almost invariably make up the pattern (or figures) of the dances.

For instance, in the first part of the Natural Turn in the Waltz the Man moves forward and round his Lady and is therefore on the outside of the 'arc' (or part of a circle), while on the last part—Steps 4, 5, 6—he is on the inner rim of the arc. The right interpretation of this idea throws light on what may appear to be complicated points of technique.

Timing and Construction of Figures. The Social Quickstep can be expressed as 'Slow, Slow, Quick, Quick' danced in varying directions. In the Quickstep, the 'Right Foot Forward', although starting as a 'Walk' (technically known as a heel-lead), really acts as a springboard to prepare the man for the rise onto the ball of his foot for the following Chasse (a shorthand term for three steps indicating Side, Close, Side), in this instance danced on the balls of his feet. Then, following the first four steps of the Quarter Turn he can either dance the Heel-Pivot which keeps him 'in-line' with his Lady and is a most useful and clever little movement for the dancer to learn (see page 56), or the alternative, which is the Progressive Chasse. This is perhaps the most characteristic figure of the dance and one which well rewards a close study of the notes, because it finishes in a foot position 'outside' the partner, but still in contact with her, of course.

It is in the execution of this figure in particular that the dancer may find it worth while to refer back to the opening theme regarding the artistic aspect of 'contact' and how best to approach this, as obviously it is not always easy to recognise this 'principle'. Other adjustments connected with these ideas are included in the descriptions of the figures.

Do not be discouraged by the exaggerated way in which the Quickstep is danced in competitions. With so much talent around, all this exaggeration is a pity and certainly unnecessary, but until the spectator becomes more discerning and the surrounding atmosphere less commercial, it appears to be unavoidable.

The best thing for the beginner to do is to observe and enjoy, but not imitate, and then to approach his own study of the Quickstep slowly.

Music. Time signature 4/4, indicating four beats to one bar of music. For descriptive purposes the timing of the figures is given in Slows and Quicks: 'Slow' represents two beats: '*One, Two*' or '*Three, Four*'; 'Quick' represents one beat: '*One*' or '*Two*'; '*Three*' or '*Four*'. Tempo recommended is 50 bars to the minute.

Hold. As Waltz.

Figures Described

1 *Quarter Turns*
2 *Progressive Chasse*
3 *Forward Lock Step*
4 *The Natural Turn with Hesitation*
5 *The Chasse Reverse Turn*
6 *The Natural Pivot Turn*
7 *Alternative ending to Chasse Reverse*
8 *Suggested Amalgamations*

1 *THE QUARTER TURNS*

Man	Timing	Lady	Timing
Commence facing diagonally wall, weight on LF		Commence backing diagonally wall, weight on RF	

	Man	Timing	Lady	Timing
1	RF forward, commencing to turn right, rising from heel-lead to ball of foot as second step moves into position	S	LF back, commencing to turn right. Ball of foot to heel	S
2	LF to side, continuing to turn to face wall. LF placed on ball of foot	Q	RF to side pointing diagonally centre, continuing turn, body facing centre. RF placed on ball of foot	Q
3	Continuing turn on ball of LF, close RF to LF on ball of foot. Backing diagonally centre, weight on RF	Q	Continuing to turn slightly in body, close LF to RF, ball of foot. Facing diagonally centre, weight on LF	Q
4	Move LF sideways backing diagonally centre (no further turn). Ball of foot lowering to heel as next step (5) is taken	S	RF diagonally forward (slightly between Man's feet) facing diagonally centre. Ball of foot lowering to heel as next step (5) is taken	S
5	RF back, commencing to turn left, releasing left toe	S	LF forward, commencing to turn left. Heel-lead to ball of foot	S
6	LF closes to RF without weight. At same time continuing to turn left on right heel	Q	Still turning, RF small step to side. Ball of foot, backing wall	Q
7	Continue to turn on right heel with slight pressure on ball of LF. End facing diagonally wall, weight on whole of RF	Q	Continue to turn on RF. Close LF to RF on ball of foot, lowering left heel as next step (8) is taken. End backing diagonally wall, weight on LF	Q
8	LF forward, heel-lead to whole foot. Facing diagonally wall*	S	RF back, backing diagonally wall	S

N.B.* Steps 5, 6, 7, 8 are known as a Heel-Pivot. The weight of the body should not be taken too quickly over the right heel on Step 6. On Step 7 the weight is on the whole of the RF as Step 8 is taken when the right heel is released.

2 *THE PROGRESSIVE CHASSE*

Precede with first four Steps of the Quarter Turn

	Man	Timing	Lady	Timing
	Commence backing diagonally centre, weight on LF		Commence facing diagonally centre, weight on RF	
1	RF back, commencing to turn left. Ball of foot to heel	S	LF forward, commencing to turn left. Heel-lead to ball of foot	S
2	LF to side, pointing diagonally wall, body facing wall. Ball of foot	Q	Continuing to turn, RF to side backing wall, ball of foot	Q
3	Slight body turn to left, RF closes to LF, body almost facing diagonally wall, feet facing diagonally wall, ball of RF	Q	Continuing turn on ball of RF, close LF to RF on ball of foot. End body almost backing diagonally wall, feet backing diagonally wall, weight on LF	Q
4	Move LF sideways and slightly forward in relation to RF preparing to step outside Lady. Ball of foot lowering as next step (5) is taken	S	Move RF sideways, backing diagonally wall. End RF side and slightly back in relation to LF. Ball of foot lowering to heel as next step (5) is taken	S
5	RF forward outside Lady, facing diagonally wall, body almost facing diagonally wall. Heel-lead to whole foot	S	LF back, partner outside. Backing diagonally wall, body almost backing diagonally wall	S

N.B. For following figure see Amalgamations.

3 *THE FORWARD LOCK STEP*

Precede with Progressive Chasse

	Man	Timing	Lady	Timing
	Commence facing diagonally wall (body almost facing diagonally wall), weight on LF		Commence backing diagonally wall, body almost backing diagonally wall, weight on RF	
1	RF forward outside Lady. Heel-lead preparing to rise to ball of foot	S	LF back, Man outside. Ball, heel LF releasing toe of RF	S
2	LF diagonally forward, ball of foot	Q	RF back, ball of foot	Q
3	RF crosses behind LF, weight on RF, ball of foot	Q	LF crosses in front of RF, ball of foot, weight on LF	Q
4	Travelling diagonally wall, LF diagonally forward, ball of foot lowering to heel as next step (5) is taken	S	RF diagonally back, ball of foot lowering to heel as next step (5) is taken	S
5	RF forward outside Lady. Heel-lead to whole foot	S	LF back	S

N.B. This figure travels in a direct line diagonally to wall.

Follow with Natural Turn outside Lady on right side. (Step 5 becomes Step 1 of the Natural Turn.)

4 *THE NATURAL TURN WITH HESITATION*

Precede with Quarter Turns or Progressive Chasse

	Man	Timing	Lady	Timing
	Commence facing diagonally wall, weight on LF		Commence backing diagonally wall, weight on RF	
1	RF forward commencing to turn right, rising from heel-lead to ball of foot as second step (LF) moves into position	S	LF back, commencing to turn right. Ball of foot to heel	S
2	LF to side, continuing to turn to back diagonally centre. LF placed on ball of foot	Q	RF to side, continuing turn pointing to LOD placed on ball of foot	Q
3	Continuing turn on ball of LF close RF to LF on ball of foot lowering right heel as next step (4) is taken. Weight on RF backing LOD	Q	Continuing turn, close LF to RF. Ball of foot lowering to heel as next step (4) is taken. Facing LOD, weight on LF	Q
4	LF back, commencing to turn right. Turn to right on left heel, at same time draw RF back and place to side of LF without weight. Facing diagonally centre	S	RF forward, continuing to turn right. At same time draw LF towards RF and, turning on ball of RF place LF to side of RF on ball of foot without weight, backing diagonally centre	S
5	Take weight onto whole of RF	S	Take weight onto ball of LF	S
6	Hesitate, weight on whole of RF releasing left heel. End facing diagonally centre	S	Lower left heel, at same time draw RF towards LF without weight (Hesitation)	S

N.B. When danced round a corner, reduce amount of turn on Steps 4, 5 and 6 to end facing diagonally centre of new LOD.

Follow with Chasse Reverse Turn.

5 *THE CHASSE REVERSE TURN*

Precede with Natural Turn with Hesitation.

	Man	Timing	Lady	Timing
	Commence facing diagonally centre, weight on RF		Commence backing diagonally centre, weight on LF	
1	LF forward commence to turn left, rising from heel-lead to ball of foot as second step moves into position	S	RF back, commence to turn left, ball of foot to heel	S
2	RF to side, continuing to turn to back diagonally wall. RF placed on ball of foot	Q	LF to side, pointing to LOD continuing turn, LF placed on ball of foot	Q
3	Continuing turn on ball of RF, close LF to RF. Ball of foot lowering to heel as next step (4) is taken. Backing LOD, weight on LF	Q	Continuing turn, close RF to LF, ball of foot lowering to heel as next step (4) is taken. Facing LOD, weight on RF	Q
4	RF back, commencing to turn left, releasing toe of LF	S	LF forward, commencing to turn left. Heel-lead to ball of foot	S
5	LF closes to RF without weight at same time continuing to turn left on right heel	Q	Still turning, RF small step to side. Ball of foot, backing wall	Q
6	Continue to turn on right heel with slight pressure on ball of LF. End facing diagonally wall with weight on whole of RF	Q	Continue to turn on RF. Close LF to RF. Ball of foot lowering left heel as next step (7) is taken. End backing diagonally wall, weight on LF	Q
7	LF forward, heel-lead to whole foot	S	RF back, backing diagonally wall	S

N.B. Steps 4, 5 and 6 are the Heel Pivot

Follow with Quarter Turns. See also Amalgamations.

6 *THE NATURAL PIVOT TURN (ROUND CORNER)*

Precede with the Quarter Turns or the Progressive Chasse

	Man	Timing	Lady	Timing
	Commence facing diagonally wall, weight on LF		Commence backing diagonally wall, weight on RF	
1	RF forward, commencing to turn right, rising from heel-lead to ball of foot as second step (LF) moves into position	S	LF back, commencing to turn right. Ball of foot to heel	S
2	LF to side, continuing turn to back diagonally centre. LF placed on ball of foot	Q	RF to side, continuing to turn, pointing to LOD. Place on ball of foot	Q
3	Continuing turn on ball of LF, close RF to LF on ball of foot, lowering right heel as next step (4) is taken. Weight on RF, backing LOD	Q	Continuing turn, close LF to RF. Ball of foot lowering to heel as next step (4) is taken. Facing LOD, weight on LF	Q
4	LF back and very slightly leftwards. Turn to right on ball of LF allowing left heel to touch the floor. Hold RF forward in direct line with LF as turn is made, then release left heel. End with weight on ball of LF, facing diagonally wall of new LOD	S	RF forward facing LOD heel-lead. Turn to right on ball of foot holding LF back. Lower heel of RF as turn is completed. End backing diagonally wall of new LOD	S
	Take weight forward to RF making this the first step of Quarter Turns		Take weight back to LF for first step of following figure	

7 *ALTERNATIVE ENDING TO FIRST 3 STEPS OF CHASSE REVERSE TURN*

Having danced Steps 1, 2 and 3 of Chasse Reverse Turn, end backing LOD, and follow with Progressive Chasse as described below:

	Man	Timing	Lady	Timing
	Commence backing LOD, weight on LF		Commence facing LOD, weight on RF	
1	RF back, commencing to turn left. Ball of foot to heel	S	LF forward, commencing to turn left. Heel-lead to ball of foot	S
2	LF to side, pointing diagonally wall. Body facing wall, ball of foot	Q	Continuing to turn, RF to side. Backing wall, ball of foot	Q
3	Slight body turn to left. RF closes to LF. Body almost facing diagonally wall, feet facing diagonally wall. Ball of RF	Q	Continuing turn on ball of RF close LF to RF on ball of foot. End body almost backing diagonally wall, feet backing diagonally wall, weight on LF	Q
4	Move LF sideways, end LF side and slightly forward in relation to RF. Preparing to step outside Lady. Ball of foot lowering as next step (5) is taken	S	Move RF sideways. End RF side and slightly back in relation to LF, body almost backing diagonally wall, feet backing diagonally wall	S
5	RF forward outside Lady, facing diagonally wall, body almost facing diagonally wall	S	LF back, partner outside, backing diagonally wall, body almost backing diagonally wall	S

N.B. For following figures see Amalgamations.

SUGGESTED AMALGAMATIONS

A Quarter Turns
Natural Turn with Hesitation
Chasse Reverse Turn

Natural Pivot Turn round corner
Quarter Turns

B First Four Steps of Quarter Turns
Progressive Chasse
Forward Lock Step
Natural Turn with Hesitation round corner
First Three Steps Chasse Reverse Turn
Progressive Chasse
Natural Pivot Turn (round corner)
First Four Steps of Quarter Turns
Progressive Chasse and Forward Lock Step

Above can be repeated, but first Step of Quarter Turn will commence outside Lady on right side.

6

QUICK WALTZ

INTRODUCTION

During almost the whole of Queen Victoria's reign, the 'Quick' or Viennese Waltz remained popular and this continued well into the 20th century, in fact until the arrival of the 'new sound' (American jazz syncopation).

This sustained popularity of the 'Quick' Waltz was undoubtedly supported—one might almost say assured—by the extraordinary amount of good music composed in its idiom: first Weber (1786–1826) with his 'Invitation to the Waltz', in which Nijinski gave an inspired and electrifying performance in Monte Carlo in 1911; then Chopin (1810–1849), whose waltz music forms the background of Les Sylphides, thus creating a vehicle for Margot Fonteyn—as well as other great artists including Anna Pavlova. There are the musical shows too, such as the 'Merry Widow' whose musical score by Franz Lehàr (1870–1948) included a waltz of universal popularity and is still 'on the road'; these are just a few of the outstanding examples of the music available.

The dance itself is known to have been created and danced by the peasantry of Southern Germany and Bavaria as early as 1780. It was called 'The Ländler' and its chief characteristic was the continuous and swift rotations and turning figures danced by the man and his partner. This was the dance that arrived in Vienna and eventually came into its own, for in the 19th century Johann Strauss and his son, also called Johann, managed between them to write hundreds of 'quick-time' waltzes, Johann Junior being responsible for the opera 'Die Fledermaus' and 'The Blue Danube'. The dance now became known as the 'Viennese

Waltz' and was danced by everyone, not only the peasantry —whether in Vienna, Paris, London or New York.

Although today the quick-time waltz is played less often than in the past, a study of the dance is useful. 'Party' and Sequence Dances very often include a few bars of waltzing (usually played at rather less than 'top' speed). Here is some advice on how to begin the practice.

1 Keep all the steps small and rather 'flat'; this may sound strange, but it makes for steadiness and timing when dancing at speed.

2 Remember that the accent is on the *first* beat: find this and let it 'carry you through' the bar. (Conductors vary in their interpretations, which can be confusing if you are trying to count 1–2–3 *and* work out figures at the same time). All the 'hesitations' are particularly useful in this respect.

The Viennese Waltz proper is beyond the scope of this book but the Quick Waltz will provide a foundation for further study in the technique should the beginner wish to improve his standard and become a more advanced dancer. (P.H.)

THE DANCE

Music. Time signature: 3/4 and 6/8. Tempo: approx 60 bars per minute.

Hold. Contact, as in Waltz, which facilitates the rotating action of two or more Natural or Reverse Turns when they are danced continuously.

Footwork. In view of the speed of the music the dancer does not rise high onto his toes.

Figures Described

1 Natural Turn
2 Reverse Turn
3 Change Steps, RF and LF
4 Forward and Backward Hesitations
5 Scissors
6 Amalgamations

SIDE HESITATIONS

For Preliminary Practice:

	Man	Lady	Timing
	Commence facing LOD, weight on LF	Commence backing LOD, weight on RF	
1	RF side, releasing left heel	LF side, releasing right heel	1
2	Rising very slightly on ball of RF, close LF towards RF keeping weight on RF	Rising slightly onto ball of LF, close RF towards LF, keeping weight on LF	2
3	Hesitate with weight on RF lowering right heel at end of 3rd beat	Hesitate with weight on LF, lowering left heel at end of 3rd beat	3
4	LF to side, releasing right heel	RF side, releasing left heel	1
5	Rising very slightly onto ball of LF, close RF towards LF keeping weight on LF	Rising very slightly onto ball of RF close LF towards RF keeping weight on RF	2
6	Hesitate with weight on LF, lowering left heel at end of 3rd beat	Hesitate with weight on RF, lowering right heel at end of 3rd beat	3

The above is a preliminary practice action in order to become accustomed to the quick tempo, and can be repeated as desired.

1 *NATURAL TURN*
Precede with LF Change Step

	Man	Lady	Timing
	Commence facing diagonally wall, weight on LF	Commence backing diagonally wall, weight on RF	
1	RF forward, commencing to turn right. Heel, ball	LF back, commencing to turn right. Ball, heel	1
2	LF side, continuing turn, backing diagonally centre. Ball of LF	RF side, pointing LOD. Ball of foot	2
3	Continuing turn on LF, RF closes to LF. End backing LOD, weight on RF. Ball, heel	Continuing turn, LF closes to RF. End facing LOD, weight on LF. Ball, heel	3
4	LF back and slightly leftwards, commencing to turn right. Ball, heel	RF forward, commencing to turn right. Heel, ball	1
5	RF small step side, pointing diagonally centre. Ball of foot.	LF side, continuing turn. Backing centre. Ball of foot	2
6	LF closes to RF, facing diagonally centre. Weight on LF. Ball, heel	RF closes to LF, backing diagonally centre. Weight on RF. Ball heel	3

Follow with RF Change Step.

2 *REVERSE TURN*
Precede with RF Change Step

	Man	Lady	Timing
	Commence facing diagonally centre, weight on RF	Commence backing diagonally centre, weight on LF	
1	LF forward, commencing to turn left. Heel, ball	RF back, commencing to turn left. Ball heel	1
2	RF side and slightly back, continuing turn. Backing diagonally wall. Ball of foot	Continuing turn, LF small step to side, pointing to LOD. Ball of foot	2

	Man	Lady	Timing
3	Continuing turn, LF *crosses* in front of RF. Backing LOD, weight on LF. Ball, heel	Continuing turn, close RF to LF facing LOD. Weight on RF. Ball of foot, lowering heel at end of step	3
4	RF back, commencing to turn left. Ball, heel	LF forward, commencing to turn left. Heel, ball	1
5	Continuing turn, LF small step side, pointing diagonally wall. Ball of foot	RF side and slightly back, continuing turn. Ball of foot	2
6	RF closes to LF continuing turn. End facing diagonally wall, weight on RF. Ball of foot lowering to heel at end of step	Continuing turn, LF *crosses* in front of RF. End backing diagonally wall, weight on LF. Ball, heel	3

Follow with LF Change Step.

3 *CHANGE STEPS*

Left Foot Change Step: precede with Reverse Turn

	Man	**Lady**	**Timing**
	Commence facing diagonally wall, weight on RF	Commencing backing diagonally wall, weight on LF	
1	LF forward. Heel, ball	RF back. Ball, heel	1
2	RF diagonally forward, ball of foot	LF diagonally back, ball of foot	2
3	LF closes to RF. End facing diagonally wall weight on LF. Ball, heel	RF closes to LF, weight on RF. Backing diagonally wall. Ball, heel	3

Follow with a Natural Turn. This Change Step can also be curved slightly to the left.

Right Foot Change Step: precede with Natural Turn

	Man	Lady	Timing
	Commence facing diagonally centre, weight on LF	Commence backing diagonally centre, weight on RF	
1	RF forward, heel, ball	LF back, ball, heel	1
2	LF diagonally forward, ball of foot	RF diagonally back. Ball of foot	2
3	RF closes to LF facing diagonally wall. Weight on RF. Ball, heel	LF closes to RF backing diagonally wall. Weight on LF. Ball, heel	3

N.B. This step can also be curved slightly to the right.

Follow with Reverse Turn.

4 *FORWARD AND BACKWARD HESITATIONS*

	Man	Lady	Timing
	Commence facing diagonally wall, weight on LF	Commence with weight on RF	
1	RF forward, heel lead	LF back, ball, heel	1
2	Release right heel, rising very slightly onto ball of RF. Close LF to RF, keeping weight on RF	Draw RF to LF, keeping weight on LF	2
3	Hesitate with weight on ball of RF, lowering right heel at end of 3rd beat as LF starts to move back	Hesitate with weight on ball of LF	3
4	LF back, ball, heel	RF forward, heel lead. Release right heel, rising very slightly onto ball of RF	1
5	Draw RF to LF, keeping weight on LF	Close LF to RF, keeping weight on RF	2
6	Hesitate with weight on ball of LF	Hesitate with weight on ball of RF lowering right heel at end of 3rd beat as LF starts to move back	3

These Forward and Backward Hesitations can be repeated

without turn or turning gradually to the right. Practise as an 8-bar phrase. Exactly the same figure can be commenced with the left foot forward and right foot back either with or without turning left.

5 *SCISSORS*

Precede with the Reverse Turn

	Man	**Lady**	**Timing**
	Commence facing diagonally wall, weight on RF	Commencing backing diagonally wall, weight on LF	
1	LF forward, commence to turn left. Heel, ball	RF back, commence to turn left. Ball, heel	1
2	Continuing to turn left, RF to side. Ball of foot	Continuing to turn, LF to side. Ball of foot	2
3	Continuing to turn on ball of RF almost close LF to RF. Prepare to step outside Lady. End facing diagonally centre, weight on LF. Ball, heel	Slight turn to left on ball of LF, RF closes towards LF, backing diagonally centre. Ball, heel	3
4	RF forward moving to centre, outside Lady, commencing to turn right. Heel, ball	LF back, commencing to turn right. Ball, heel	1
5	Continuing to turn, LF to side, ball of foot	Continuing to turn, RF to side. Ball of foot	2
6	Turning to right on ball of LF almost close RF to LF. Ball, heel. End facing diagonally wall, weight on RF, preparing to step to left side of Lady	Turning to right on ball of RF, LF almost closes to RF. Ball, heel. End backing diagonally wall, weight on LF	3
7	LF forward to left side of Lady, commencing to turn left. Heel, ball	RF back, commencing to turn left. Ball, heel	1
8	Continuing to turn, RF to side. Ball of foot	LF to side. Ball of foot	2
9	Turning on ball of RF almost close LF to RF preparing to step outside Lady. Ball, heel. End facing diagonally centre or diagonally wall of new LOD.	Slight turn to left on ball of LF, RF almost closes to LF, weight on RF. End backing diagonally centre or diagonally wall of new LOD	3

Follow with Natural Turn commenced outside Lady or Forward Hesitation commenced outside Lady.

AMALGAMATIONS

A Commence facing diagonally wall
RF Forward and Backward Hesitation. Natural Turn
RF Change Step
Reverse Turn. LF Change Step
These can be repeated

B Commence facing diagonally centre
LF Forward Hesitation
RF Backward Hesitation turning left
LF Forward Hesitation
RF Backward Hesitation turning left
LF Forward Hesitation, end backing diagonally centre
(Man will have turned approximately half a turn)
Steps 4, 5 and 6 of Reverse Turn, end facing LOD
Reverse Turn, end facing diagonally wall
LF Change Step

C Commence facing diagonally centre
RF Change Step
Reverse Turn, end diagonally wall
The Scissors, end diagonally centre
Natural Turn, commenced outside Lady, diagonally centre
(If danced round corner the Natural Turn would commence diagonally wall)

7

RUMBA

INTRODUCTION

Today the Rumba, as danced in the social ballroom or in competitions, is fairly well standardised and uniform in pattern. But this does not mean that the Rumba has always been a distinct and clearly categorised dance; in fact, its origin and evolution is a complicated story.

The word 'rumba' is really a generic term, covering a variety of names, of which Afro-Cuban, Son, Son-Montuno, Danzon, Guajira, Mambo, Conga, Guaracha, Nanigo, are but a few. The names of the dances come from many sources and one must not attempt any literal translations: for instance, 'son' in Spanish simply means 'sound'.

There are two basic sources of the dances: one Spanish, the other African. Although the main growth was in Cuba, there were similar dance developments which took place in the other Caribbean islands and in Latin America generally. The 'rumba influence' came in the 16th century with the black slaves imported from Africa. The dance was inspired by the walk of the cock and hence showed a similarity to the Chilean national folk dance—the 'Cueca'. In its first, primitive form, it rather scandalised the whites, and therefore underwent a 'refining' process over the years. It was danced to a syncopated rhythm which 'attacked' on the *second* beat of the music.

In Spain, the 'Bolero' was a very old dance, which became considerably modified in its incorporation into the Cuban dancing. It became known as the 'Criollabolero' (Criolla = Creole). Today, you can hear talk of the 'Rumba', the 'Son' and the 'Bolero', without the users of these terms having much idea as to how they came about.

The dances are all rhythmically similar but vary considerably in tempo. In Latin America and the USA the Rumba is a fast dance, the Son of medium tempo, and the Bolero slow.

Between 1920 and 1950 the Cuban dance-halls were invaded by American-type jazz and boogie-woogie. It is clear that the American-type syncopation was assimilated into the rhythms of the Rumba, creating new and hybrid forms of Cuban jazz.

Basically the Rumba is the spirit and soul of Latin American music and dance: it has completely fascinating rhythms and bodily expressions which enable the lady dancer to express her grace and femininity and the man to show her off in this way while himself feeling the spell of the music and the sheer joy of being alive.

Whatever its origin, and however it evolved, the Rumba as it is danced in ballrooms today in most countries around the world, is enjoyable, rhythmic, attractive and easy to learn.

In Europe, the introduction of Latin American dancing—and the Rumba in particular—owed much to the enthusiasm and interpretative ability of Monsieur Pierre, who became London's leading teacher in this dance form.

Pierre was a Basque, and a skilled ballroom dancer and teacher. In the 1930's, with his partner, Doris Lavelle, he demonstrated and popularised Latin American dancing in London. Up to the mid-1940's the accepted Rumba was that evolved and practised in the USA—the 'Square Rumba'.

Pierre and Lavelle introduced the true 'Cuban Rumba', danced on the second beat, but this was not accepted without much argument and was only finally established, through Pierre's efforts, as the officially recognised version, in 1955.

(G.W.)

The Music. This is written in 4/4 time, 4 beats to a bar of music, and each beat should be given its full value—one for the first step, one for the second step and two for the third step. The tempo is 28–31 bars per minute, the slower tempo being popular as it gives more time to 'feel' the rhythm and to dance without effort.

Footwork, Hold and Action. The basic action of the Rumba should be a soft flexing and straightening of the knees, with a rhythmical hip movement. It is not a difficult dance to learn, once the basic rhythm is understood. The rhythm should be expressed through the feet, legs and hips, without any tendency to exaggeration.

Each step is taken on the ball of the foot with a flexed knee: when weight is taken onto the foot the heel lowers and the knee straightens: the heel of the other foot is now released and the knee is flexed. At this point the hips move gently to the side of the straightened leg.

The stance is erect without stiffness, the partners' bodies being well balanced, standing facing each other about 6 in. (15 cm) apart. The man should hold the lady's right hand with his left at shoulder level, with her fingers between his thumb and first finger. His right hand is placed high on the lady's shoulder blade, and her left hand rests lightly on his right upper arm.

Alignments are given purely for ease in learning. As the Rumba is a non-progressive dance, the figures may be commenced and finished in any alignment.

The first step of the Basic Movement—left foot forward—is taken on the second beat in the Cuban Rumba. It is found to be easier if, to commence the dance, one takes a step to the side on the right foot and moves the hips gently to the right on the first beat.

Figures Described

1 *Basic Movement*
2 *Side Step*
3 *Natural Top*
4 *Cucarachas to Left and Right*
5 *Progressive Walks Forward and Backward*
6 *Side Rock*
7 *Shoulder to Shoulder*
8 *New York*
9 *Alemana Turn (Under arm turn to Right)*
10 *Hand to Hand*
11 *Alternative Basic Movement*

1 *BASIC MOVEMENT*

Commence in Normal Hold, feet apart or closed

	Man	Lady	Timing
	Facing wall; weight on RF	Facing centre; weight on LF	
1	LF forward	RF back	2
2	Replace weight to RF	Replace weight to LF	3
3	LF to side and slightly back	RF to side	4 1
4	RF back	LF forward	2
5	Replace weight to LF	Replace weight to RF	3
6	RF to side	LF to side and slightly back	4 1

A gradual turn to the Left is made throughout. May also be danced without turn. May be repeated.

2 *SIDE STEP*

Commence in Normal Hold, feet apart or closed. Precede with Basic Movement

	Man	Lady	Timing
	Facing wall. Weight on RF	Facing centre. Weight on LF	
1	LF to side	RF to side	2
2	Close RF to LF	Close LF to RF	3
3–6	Repeat steps 1 and 2 twice. LRLR	Repeat steps 1 and 2 twice. RLRL	4 1 2 3 4 1

May be danced without turn or with a gradual turn to the Left in a circular pattern. Follow with Basic Movement or Cucarachas.

3 *NATURAL TOP*

Commence in Normal Hold, feet apart. Precede with 1–3 of the Basic Movement without turn

	Man	Lady	Timing
	Facing LOD. Weight on LF.	Backing LOD. Weight on RF	
1	RF behind LF, toe to heel, toe turned out, commencing to turn to Right	LF to side, commencing to turn to Right	2
2	LF to side. Continuing to turn to Right	RF in front of LF, toe turned out, continuing to turn to Right	3
3	Close RF to LF	LF to side	4 1

Follow with Basic Movement or Side Step.

4 *CUCARACHAS TO LEFT AND RIGHT*

A. Side Cucaracha to Left:

Commence in Normal Hold. Precede with Side Step

	Man	Lady	Timing
	Facing wall: weight on RF	Facing centre: weight on LF	
1	LF to side with part weight	RF to side with part weight	2
2	Replace weight to RF	Replace weight to LF	3
3	LF closes to RF	RF closes to LF	4 1

Follow with Side Cucaracha to Right

N.B. Step 1 may be danced diagonally back

B. Side Cucaracha to Right:

Commence in Normal Hold. Precede with Side Cucaracha to Left.

	Man	Lady	Timing
	Facing wall: weight on LF	Facing centre, weight on RF	
1	RF to side with part weight	LF to side with part weight	2
2	Replace weight to LF	Replace weight to RF	3
3	RF closes to LF	LF closes to RF	4 1

Follow with Basic Movement.

N.B. Step 1 may be danced diagonally back.

5 *PROGRESSIVE WALKS FORWARD AND BACKWARD*

These are steps danced in groups of 3 or 6, taken forward or backward. Forward Walks normally commence after 1–6 of the Basic Movement, stepping forward on RF on Step 6. Lady LF back. Backward Walks commence after 1–3 of the Basic Movement, stepping back on LF on Step 3. Lady RF forward. Follow Forward Walks with Basic Movement and Backward Walks with 4–6 of Basic Movement.

6 *SIDE ROCK*

Commence in Normal Hold. Precede with 1–3 of Basic Movement.

	Man	**Lady**	**Timing**
	Facing LOD. Weight on LF	Backing LOD. Weight on RF	
1	RF to side	LF to side	2
2	Replace weight to LF	Replace weight to RF	3
3	Replace weight to RF	Replace weight to LF	4 1

Follow with New York or Basic Movement.

7 *SHOULDER TO SHOULDER*

Commence in Normal Hold with feet apart. Precede with Basic Movement.

	Man	**Lady**	**Timing**
	Facing diagonally wall. Weight on RF, slightly forward, preparing to step outside Lady on Left side	Backing diagonally wall. Weight on LF	
1	LF forward outside partner on Left side	RF back	2
2	Replace weight to RF	Replace weight to LF outside partner on Left side	3
3	LF to side and slightly forward, turning ¼ to Left	RF to side and slightly back, turning ¼ to Left	4 1
4	RF forward outside partner	LF back	2

Man	Lady	Timing
5 Replace weight to LF	Replace weight to RF outside partner	3
6 RF to side and slightly forward, turning ¼ to Right	LF to side and slightly back, turning ¼ to Right	4 1
7–12 Steps 1–6 may be repeated, turning square to partner on last step		2 3 4 1 2 3 4 1

Follow with Side Step or Basic Movement.

8 *NEW YORK*

Commence in Normal Hold, feet apart. Precede with Side Rock or Basic Movement.

Man	Lady	Timing
Facing LOD. Weight on RF	Backing LOD. Weight on LF	
1 LF forward in Left Side-by-side position, turning ¼ to the Right, releasing hold with right hand	RF forward, turning ¼ to Left, releasing left hand	2
2 Replace weight to RF	Replace weight to LF	3
3 LF to side, turning ¼ to Left, taking Lady's left hand in right hand and releasing hold with left hand	RF to side, turning ¼ to Right, releasing right hand	4 1
4 RF forward in Right Side-by-side position, turning ¼ to Left	LF forward, turning ¼ to Right	2
5 Replace weight to LF	Replace weight to RF	3
6 RF to side, turning ¼ to Right, taking Lady's right hand in left hand and releasing hold with right hand	LF to side, turning¼ to Left, releasing left hand	4 1
Finish facing LOD	Finish backing LOD	
Steps 1-6 may be repeated.		

N.B. Less turn may be made to take step 1 in Closed Promenade Position and step 4 in Promenade Position.

Follow with Basic Movement or Alternative Basic Movement.

9 *ALEMANA TURN* (*Lady's Under Arm Turn*)

Commence in Normal Hold. Precede with Basic Movement.

	Man	Lady	Timing
	Facing wall, weight on RF	Backing wall, weight on LF	
1	LF forward	RF back	2
2	Replace weight to RF, commencing to raise left arm	LF forward	3
3	LF closes to RF, commencing to lead Lady to turn to Right	RF forward, commencing to turn Right	4 1
4	RF back, leading Lady to turn to Right under left arm, releasing hold with right hand	LF forward, turning Right under right arm, releasing left hand	2
5	Replace weight to LF, continuing to turn Lady under left arm	RF forward, still turning under right arm	3
6	RF closes to LF, lowering left arm and taking normal hold	LF forward, having completed one turn to Right over Steps 3–6, lowering right arm and taking Normal Hold	4 1

N.B. When followed by Hand-to-Hand, Step 6 will be to side, taking Double Hold.

Follow with Basic Movement or Hand-to-Hand.

10 *HAND TO HAND*

Commence in Double Hold, feet apart. Precede with Alemana Turn.

	Man	Lady	Timing
	Facing wall. Weight on RF	Backing wall. Weight on LF	
1	LF back in Right Side-by-Side Position, turning $\frac{1}{4}$ turn to Left, releasing hold with left hand	RF back, turning $\frac{1}{4}$ to Right, releasing hold with right hand	2
2	Replace weight to RF	Replace weight to LF	3
3	LF to side, turning $\frac{1}{4}$ to Right, taking Lady's right hand in left hand	RF to side, turning $\frac{1}{4}$ to Left	4 1

	Man	Lady	Timing
4	RF back in Left Side-by-side position, turning ¼ to Right, releasing hold with right hand	LF back, turning ¼ to Left, releasing hold with left hand	2
5	Replace weight to LF	Replace weight to RF	3
6	RF to side, turning ¼ to Left	LF to side, turning ¼ to Right	4 1
	Finish facing wall	Finish backing wall	

N.B. From the time that the Man takes Double Hold at the end of the preceding step, both arms should be kept steady.

Steps 1–6 may be repeated. Follow with Basic Movement or Alternative Basic Movement.

11 *ALTERNATIVE BASIC MOVEMENT*

Commence in Normal Hold, feet apart. Precede with Hand to Hand or New York.

	Man	Lady	Timing
	Facing wall, or LOD, weight on RF	Backing wall, or LOD, weight on LF	
1	Close LF to RF	Close RF to LF	2
2	Replace weight on RF	Replace weight on LF	3
3	LF to side	RF to side	4 1
4	Close RF to LF	Close LF to RF	2
5	Replace weight to LF	Replace weight to RF	3
6	RF to side	LF to side	4 1

Follow with Basic Movement.

SUGGESTED AMALGAMATIONS

1 Basic Movement; Shoulder to Shoulder; Side Step (Turning); Cucaracha to Left; Cucaracha to Right.

2 First half Basic Movement; 6 Backward Progressive Walks; Natural Top; first half Basic Movement; Side Rock; New York.

3 Alemana Turn; Hand to Hand; Alternative Basic Movement; Basic Movement.

4 Basic Movement; New York; Alternative Basic Movement; Basic Movement.
5 First half of Basic Movement; Natural Top; Side Step; Basic Movement.
6 Basic Movement; Side Step; Cucaracha to Left; Cucaracha to Right; Basic Movement.
7 Basic Movement; New York; Side Step (Turning).

8

SAMBA

INTRODUCTION

The Samba is an animated dance with a strong and characteristic rhythm. It originated in Africa and was taken to Bahia in the north of Brasil by the slaves sent to work on the sugar plantations. The dance gradually lost its ritualistic nature and eventually became the Brasilian national dance.

It was Carnival Time in Rio de Janeiro that first put the Samba on the Western map. The Bahians and others from the sugar plantations and villages travelled to Rio for the yearly festivities. Gradually the subtle beat and interpretative nuances of the Samba began to take over in the street dancing, the cafés and the ballrooms until, eventually, it became the musical and dancing soul of Brasil.

Originally, the dance had very characteristic hand movements, derived from its ritualistic function, when small containers of aromatic herbs were held in each hand and moved in front of the nose to 'drug' the dancer with the exciting fragrance. There was much solo work and, before it became a ballroom dance, it contained steps incorporated from the Indian 'Maxixe' (pronounced as 'Mah-chee-chay').

The great American dancers, Irene and Vernon Castle, used the Samba in their professional routines, and so it began to spread. But it was probably Carmen Miranda, the best known Brasilian of them all, who, with her tremendous vitality and showmanship, gave the Samba its established place as one of the most exciting and catching rhythms in the world. In Brasil the 'Samba Schools' grow and flourish and the country has now developed its own balletic art which has the Samba rhythm and basic movements as a marked contribution. (G.W.)

THE DANCE

Music. This is written in 2/4 time, 2 beats to a bar of music, counted 'one, two'. In the Side, Natural and Reverse Basic Movements one beat is given to each step. In the Side, Natural and Reverse Alternative Basic Movements, counted 'one *a* two' ('*a*' denotes the quarter beat), 3/4 of a beat is given to the first step, ¼ of a beat to the second step and 1 beat to the third step.

The Corta Jaca differs in timing from the other figures. One beat is given for the first step and half beats for Steps 2—7, counted 'One, two and one and two and'. The tempo is 48–56 bars per minute.

Hold. Similar to the Rumba.

Footwork. All steps are taken Ball Flat except the quarter beat steps which are taken on the ball of the foot only. The footwork of the Corta Jaca is given in the description of the figure and differs from all other figures. The term 'part weight' denotes that weight is taken only momentarily on the foot as the next step is taken.

Knee Action. The Basic Bounce and Alternative Basic Bounce, so typical of the Samba, come from the flexing and straightening of the knees, with a slight elevation at the end of each beat of music.

In the basic bounce, with two steps to a bar of music, counted 'one, two', the knees are flexed when weight is taken on the stepping foot, and the straightening takes place between each step.

In the Alternative Basic Bounce, three steps to a bar of music, counted 1 *a* 2, the knees are flexed when weight is taken on the stepping foot, first step, straightened on the second step, flexed on the third step, straightening between this and the following step.

Figures Described. As several of the figures in the Samba are progressive it is preferable to take these moving around the room. Suggested alignments are given with all figures.

1 *Basic Movements (Natural and Alternative: Reverse and Alternative)*
2 *Side Basic Movement*
3 *Progressive Basic Movement*
4 *Whisks to Right and Left*
5 *Samba Walks in Promenade Position*
6 *Rhythm Bounce*
7 *Volta Movements*
8 *Side Samba Walks*
9 *Stationary Samba Walks*
10 *Bota Fogos*
11 *Corta Jaca*
12 *Reverse Turn*

1 *BASIC MOVEMENTS (NATURAL AND ALTERNATIVE)*

A. Natural Basic Movement:

Commence in Normal Hold, using Basic Bounce.

	Man	Lady	Timing
	Facing LOD, weight on LF	Backing LOD, weight on RF	
1	RF forward	LF back	1
2	LF closes to RF with pressure, without weight	RF closes to LF, with pressure, without weight	2
3	LF back	RF forward	1
4	RF closes to LF, with pressure, without weight	LF closes to RF, with pressure without weight	2

A gradual turn to the Right is made throughout. May also be danced without turn.

B. Natural Alternative Basic Movement:

Commence in Normal Hold, using Alternative Basic Bounce

	Man	Lady	Timing
	Facing LOD, weight on LF	Backing LOD, weight on RF	
1	RF forward	LF back	1
2	LF closes to RF	RF closes to LF	a
3	Replace weight to RF	Replace weight to LF	2
4	LF back	RF forward	1
5	RF closes to LF	LF closes to RF	a
6	Replace weight to LF	Replace weight to RF	2

N.B. Basic Natural Movements may be danced in any alignment.

A gradual turn to the Right is made throughout. May also be danced without turn.

C. Reverse Basic Movement:
Commence in Normal Hold, using Basic Bounce.

	Man	Lady	Timing
	Facing LOD, weight on RF	Backing LOD, weight on LF	
1	LF forward	RF back	1
2	RF closes to LF, with pressure without weight	LF closes to RF, with pressure, without weight	2
3	RF back	LF forward	1
4	LF closes to RF, with pressure without weight	RF closes to LF, with pressure, without weight	2

A gradual turn to the Left is made throughout. May also be danced without turn.

D. Reverse Alternative Basic Movement:
Commence in Normal Hold, using Alternative Basic Bounce.

	Man	Lady	Timing
	Facing LOD, weight on RF	Backing LOD, weight on LF	
1	LF forward	RF back	1
2	RF closes to LF	LF closes to RF	a
3	Replace weight to LF	Replace weight to RF	2
4	RF back	LF forward	1
5	LF closes to RF	RF closes to LF	a
6	Replace weight to RF	Replace weight to LF	2

N.B. Reverse Basic Movements may be danced in any alignment.

A gradual turn to the Left is made throughout. May also be danced without turn.

2 *SIDE BASIC MOVEMENT*

A. With Basic Bounce:

Commence in Normal Hold.

	Man	Lady	Timing
	Facing wall, weight on RF	Backing wall, weight on LF	
1	LF to side	RF to side	1
2	RF closes to LF, with pressure, without weight	LF closes to RF, with pressure, without weight	2
3	RF to side	LF to side	1
4	LF closes to RF, with pressure, without weight	RF closes to LF, with pressure without weight	2

B. With Alternative Basic Bounce:

Commence in Normal Hold.

	Man	Lady	Timing
	Facing wall, weight on RF	Backing wall, weight on LF	
1	LF to side	RF to side	1
2	RF closes to LF	LF closes to RF	a
3	Replace weight to LF	Replace weight to RF	2
4	RF to side	LF to side	1
5	LF closes to RF	RF closes to LF	a
6	Replace weight to RF	Replace weight to LF	2

3 *PROGRESSIVE BASIC MOVEMENT*

Commence in Normal Hold, using slight Basic Bounce. Precede with Natural Basic Movement.

	Man	Lady	Timing
	Facing diagonally wall or LOD, weight on LF	Backing diagonally wall or LOD, weight on RF	
1	RF forward	LF back	1
2	LF closes to RF with pressure, without weight	RF closes to LF with pressure, without weight	2

	Man	Lady	Timing
3	LF to side	RF to side	1
4	RF closes to LF with pressure, without weight	LF closes to RF with pressure, without weight	2

Follow with Natural Basic Movement or Corta Jaca.

4 *WHISKS*

A. Whisk to Right:

Commence in Normal Hold, using Alternative Basic Bounce. Precede with Natural Basic Movement or Whisk to Left.

	Man	Lady	Timing
	Facing wall, weight on LF	Backing wall, weight on RF	
1	RF to side	LF to side	1
2	LF behind RF, toe to heel, toe slightly turned out	RF behind LF, toe to heel, toe slightly turned out	a
3	Replace weight to RF	Replace weight to LF	2

Follow with Reverse Basic Movement, Rhythm Bounce, Whisk to Left, or Samba Walks, turning to Promenade Position to face LOD on the Whisk.

B. Whisk to Left:

Commence in Normal Hold, using Alternative Basic Bounce. Precede with Reverse Basic Movement, Whisk to Right, Samba Walks in Promenade Position, turning to face wall on the Whisk.

	Man	Lady	Timing
	Facing wall, weight on RF	Backing wall, weight on LF	
1	LF to side	RF to side	1
2	RF behind LF, toe to heel, toe slightly turned out	LF behind RF, toe to heel, toe slightly turned out	a
3	Replace weight to LF	Replace weight to RF	2

5 *SAMBA WALKS IN PROMENADE POSITION*

Commence in Promenade Position, with feet pointing to LOD. Use very slight Alternative Basic Bounce. Precede with Whisk to Right, or Side Basic Movement turning to Promenade Position.

	Man	Lady	Timing
	Facing LOD, weight on RF	Facing LOD, weight on LF	
1	LF forward	RF forward	1
2	RF back, small step, part weight	LF back, small step, part weight	a
3	Draw LF slightly towards RF	Draw RF slightly towards LF	2
4	RF forward	LF forward	1
5	LF back, small step, part weight	RF back, small step, part weight	a
6	Draw RF slightly towards LF	Draw LF slightly towards RF	2

Steps 1–6 may be repeated. End in Promenade Position. Follow with Side Basic Movement or Whisk to Left, turning to face partner.

1–3 are the LF Samba walk, 4–6 are the RF Samba walk.

6 *RHYTHM BOUNCE*

Commence in Normal Hold. Precede with Whisk to Right.

	Man	Lady	Timing
	Facing wall, weight on RF	Backing wall, weight on LF	
1	LF to side and slightly back, right knee bent and veering towards left knee	RF to side and slightly back, left knee bent and veering towards right knee	1
2–7	Keep feet in place and with a slight bounce action, swing hips slightly to— RLRLRL	Just as for Man but LRLRLR	a 2 a 1 a 2

Follow with Whisk to Right or Volta to Right.

7 VOLTA MOVEMENTS

A. Volta Turning to Left:

Commence in Normal Hold, slightly apart, using Alternative Basic Bounce. Precede with Volta to Right or Whisk to Right.

	Man	Lady	Timing
	Facing wall, weight on RF	Backing wall, weight on LF	
1	LF in front of RF, heel to toe, left toe turned out	RF in front of LF, heel to toe, right toe turned out	1
2	RF to side and slightly back, toe turned out	LF to side and slightly back, toe turned out	a
3	Draw LF in front of RF, heel to toe, left toe turned out	Draw RF in front of LF, heel to toe, right toe turned out	2
4–7	Repeat Steps 2 and 3 twice	Repeat Steps 2 and 3 twice	a 1 a 2

A gradual turn, up to ¼, is made throughout. May also be danced without turn. Follow with Whisk to Right or Volta to Right.

B. Volta Turning to Right:

Commence in Normal Hold, slightly apart, using Alternative Basic Bounce. Precede with Rhythm Bounce or Volta to Left.

	Facing wall, weight on LF	Backing wall, weight on RF	
1	RF in front of LF, heel to toe, right toe turned out	LF in front of RF, heel to toe, left toe turned out	1
2	LF to side and slightly back, toe turned out	RF to side and slightly back, toe turned out	a
3	Draw RF in front of LF, heel to toe, right toe turned out	Draw LF in front of RF, heel to toe, left toe turned out	2
4–7	Repeat Steps 2 and 3 twice	Repeat Steps 2 and 3 twice	a 1 a 2

A gradual turn, up to ¼, is made throughout. May also be danced without turn. Follow with Whisk to Left or Volta to Left.

C. Spot Volta to Right:

Commence in Normal Hold, using Alternative Basic Bounce. Precede with Reverse Basic Movement, Stationary Samba Walks or Whisk to Right.

	Man	**Lady**	**Timing**
	Facing wall or LOD, weight on RF	Backing wall or LOD, weight on LF	
1	Whisk to Left—LRL, raising left arm, releasing hold with	RF in front of LF, heel to toe, right toe turned out, turning under right arm to right, releasing left hand	1
2	right hand, and turning Lady a complete	LF to side and slightly back, still turning	a
3	turn under arm to right	RF in front of LF, heel to toe, having completed a full turn to right The ball of the RF remains on one spot	2

Finish in Normal Hold. Follow with Whisk to Right or Natural Basic Movement.

D. Spot Volta to Left:

Commence in Normal Hold, using Alternative Basic Bounce. Precede with Natural Basic Movement or Whisk to Left.

	Facing wall or LOD, weight on LF	Backing wall or LOD, weight on RF	
1	Whisk to Right—RLR, raising left arm, releasing hold with	LF in front of RF, heel to toe, left toe turned out, turning under right arm to left, releasing left hand	1
2	right hand, and turning Lady a complete	RF to side and slightly back, still turning	a
3	turn under arm to left	LF in front of RF, heel to toe, having completed a full turn to left The ball of the LF remains on one spot	2

Finish in Normal Hold. Follow with Whisk to Left or Reverse Basic Movement.

8 *SIDE SAMBA WALK*

Commence in Promenade Position with feet pointing to LOD. Use very slight Alternative Basic Bounce. Precede with LF Samba Walk in Promenade Position.

	Man	**Lady**	**Timing**
	Facing LOD, weight on LF	Facing LOD, weight on RF	
1	RF forward	LF forward	1
2	LF to side with part weight	RF to side with part weight	a
3	Draw RF slightly towards LF	Draw LF slightly towards RF	2
	Follow with Samba Walk in Promenade Position on LF	Follow with Samba Walk in Promenade Position on RF	

9 *STATIONARY SAMBA WALKS*

Commence in Normal Hold. Use very slight Alternative Basic Bounce. Precede with Whisks to Left and Right.

	Man	**Lady**	**Timing**
	Facing wall or LOD	Facing centre or backing LOD	
1	LF closes to RF	RF closes to LF	1
2	RF back, part weight	LF back, part weight	a
3	Draw LF slightly towards RF	Draw RF slightly towards LF	2
4	RF closes to LF, slightly forward	LF closes to RF, slightly forward	1
5	LF back, part weight	RF back, part weight	a
6	Draw RF slightly towards LF	Draw LF slightly towards RF	2

Follow with Whisk to Left or Reverse Basic Movement.

10 *BOTA FOGOS*

A. Bota Fogos to Promenade Position and Counter Promenade Position:

Commence in Normal Hold, using Alternative Basic Bounce. Precede with Reverse Basic Movement or Reverse Turn.

	Man	Lady	Timing
	Facing wall, weight on RF	Backing wall, weight on LF	
1	LF forward	RF back	1
2	RF to side with part weight, commencing to turn to left	LF to side with part weight, commencing to turn right	a
3	Replace weight to LF in Promenade Position, continue turning to complete 1/8 over Steps 2 and 3	Replace weight to RF in Promenade Position, continue turning to complete 1/8 over Steps 2 and 3	2
4	RF forward and across in Promenade Position	LF forward and across in Promenade Position	1
5	LF to side with part weight, commencing to turn to right	RF to side with part weight, commencing to turn left	a
6	Replace weight to RF in Counter Promenade Position, continue turning to complete ¼ over Steps 5 and 6	Replace weight to LF in Counter Promenade Position, continue turning to complete ¼ over Steps 5 and 6	2
7	LF forward and across in Counter Promenade Position	RF forward and across in Counter Promenade Position	1
8	RF to side with part weight, commencing to turn to left	LF to side with part weight, commencing to turn right	a
9	Replace weight to LF in Promenade Position, continue turning to complete 3/8 to left over Steps 8 and 9	Replace weight to RF in Promenade Position, continue turning to complete 3/8 over Steps 8 and 9	2
	Follow with Samba Walk in Promenade Position on RF	Follow with Samba Walk in Promenade Position on LF	

B. Travelling Bota Fogo:
Commence in Normal Hold, using Alternative Basic Bounce. Precede with Reverse Basic Movement or Reverse Turn.

	Man	Lady	Timing
	Facing diagonally wall, weight on RF	Backing diagonally wall, weight on LF	
1	LF forward, commencing to turn to left	RF back, commencing to turn to left	1
2	RF to side with part weight, continue turning to left	LF to side with part weight, continue turning to left	a
3	Replace weight to LF to complete ¼ turn over Steps 1 to 3	Replace weight to RF to complete ¼ turn over Steps 1 to 3	2
4	RF forward outside partner, commencing to turn to right	LF back, commencing to turn to right	1
5	LF to side with part weight, continue turning to right	RF to side with part weight, continue turning to right	a
6	Replace weight to RF to complete ¼ turn over Steps 4 to 6	Replace weight to LF to complete ¼ turn over Steps 4 to 6	2
7–9	Repeat Steps 1 to 3	Repeat Steps 1 to 3	1 a 2

Follow with Natural Basic Movement, first Step outside partner, turning to face each other on Step 2

11 *CORTA JACA*

Commence in Normal Hold, no Bounce. Precede with Natural Basic Movement or Progressive Basic Movement.

	Man	Lady	Timing
	Facing wall, weight on LF	Backing wall, weight on RF	
1	RF forward, strong step	LF back	1
2	LF forward and slightly to side on heel	RF back and slightly to side on toe	2
3	RF slides leftwards, foot flat	LF slides rightwards, foot flat	and
4	LF back and slightly to side on toe	RF forward and slightly to side on heel	1

Man	Lady	Timing
5 RF slides leftwards, foot flat	LF slides rightwards, foot flat	and
6 LF forward and slightly to side on heel	RF back and slightly to side on toe	2
7 RF slides leftwards, foot flat	LF slides rightwards, foot flat	and

Finish with Steps 3 and 4 of Natural Basic Movement. Follow with Natural Basic Movement or Whisk to Right.

12 *REVERSE TURN*

Commence in Normal Hold, using Alternative Basic Bounce. Precede with Reverse Basic Movement.

Man	Lady	Timing
Facing LOD or diagonally centre	Backing LOD or diagonally centre	
1 LF forward, commencing to turn to left	RF back commencing to turn to left	
2 RF to side and slightly back, continuing to turn to left	Left heel close to right heel continuing to turn to left	a
3 LF crosses in front of RF, toe turned out, continuing to turn to left	RF closes to LF continuing to turn to left	2
4 RF back and slightly rightwards, continuing to turn to left	LF forward continuing to turn to left	1
5 Left heel close to right heel, continuing to turn to left	RF to side and slightly back continuing to turn to left	a
6 RF closes to LF, continuing to turn to left	LF crosses in front of RF, toe turned out continuing to turn to left	2

N.B. 7/8 turn or less is made over Steps 1–6; or Steps 1–6 may be repeated and one complete turn made over Steps 1–12. Follow with Reverse Basic Movement or Travelling Bota Fogos.

SUGGESTED AMALGAMATIONS

1 Reverse Basic Movement; Side Basic Movement, turning to face LOD; 4 Samba Walks in Promenade Position; Side Basic Movement, turning to face wall.

2 Whisks to Left and Right; Rhythm Bounce; Volta to Right; Volta to Left; Natural Basic Movement.

3 Whisk to Right, turning to Promenade Position to face LOD; 1 Samba Walk; 1 Side Samba Walk; 1 Samba Walk; 1 Side Samba Walk; 2 Samba Walks; Whisk to Left, turning to face wall; Natural Basic Movement.

4 Reverse Turn, to face wall; Whisks to Left and Right; 2 Stationary Samba Walks; Spot Volta to Right; Whisk to Right; Reverse Basic Movement.

5 Progressive Basic Movement, danced twice to face wall; Corta Jaca; Natural Basic Movement.

6 Reverse Basic Movement; Reverse Turn, to face LOD; Travelling Bota Fogos; Natural Basic Movement.

7 Reverse Basic Movement; Bota Fogos to Promenade and Counter Promenade Position; 3 Samba Walks in Promenade position; Whisk to Left, turning to face wall; Whisk to Right; Reverse Basic Movement.

9

PASO DOBLE

INTRODUCTION

The Paso Doble originated in Spain, the basic steps being essentially a type of march, or One-step, expressing the music which was composed to embody the colour and excitement of the bull ring.

Nevertheless, France was the country where the Paso Doble was developed in the ordinary social ballrooms. A simple version was danced in various parts of France but particularly in the southern region bordering on Spain. The French seemed to have a penchant for simplifying these dances and reducing them to a few rhythmic steps.

Several figures have French names. The first, and simplest figure, is named '*sur place*' and means 'on the spot'; '*déplacement*' means 'displacing, moving or transferring'; '*huit*' means the number eight and the figure with this name has eight steps; '*écart*' comes from the word '*écarter*' and means 'to separate'; '*appel*' means a call (the Matador's call to the bull). (G.W.)

THE DANCE

Music. This is written in 2/4 time, one beat for each step, which should be well accented. The tempo is 60–62 bars per minute.

Footwork and Hold. In the dancing, the man assumes the role of the Matador and the Lady represents his cape, therefore he should adopt a proud-looking and strong stance. The feet should be used firmly, with the knees very slightly flexed, but there should be full control over the muscles of the legs.

The footwork is heel flat for forward steps, ball flat for backward steps, ball of foot or ball flat for side steps and closing steps.

Any exceptions will be mentioned in the description of the figure.

The hold is closer than in Rumba and Samba, but is widened when dancing promenade figures.

Figures Described. In the Paso Doble many of the figures are progressive and therefore are danced moving around the room. Suggested alignments are given with all figures.

1 *Sur Place*
2 *Basic Movement*
3 *Appel*
4 *Attack*
5 *Chasses to Right and Left (with or without Elevation)*
6 *The Drag*
7 *Promenade Link*
8 *Separation*
9 *Separation with Lady's Caping Walks*
10 *The Huit (Cape)*
11 *Ecart (Fallaway Whisk) and Promenade Link to Right*

1 *SUR PLACE*

A series of 4 or 8 steps, danced in Normal Hold, replacing the weight from one foot to the other, on the balls of the feet. The heels may be lowered lightly, and the knees are very slightly flexed. May be danced with or without turn, each step taking one beat of music. Lady dances the normal opposite. The man will start with his RF, the Lady with her LF.

2 *BASIC MOVEMENT*

A series of 4 or 8 forward or backward steps, danced in Normal Hold, on the balls of the feet. The heels may be lowered lightly and the knees are very slightly flexed. May be danced with or without turn, each step taking one beat of music. Lady dances the normal opposite. The Man will start with his RF, the Lady with her LF.

3 *APPEL*

This is a firm step, danced on either foot, with foot flat and using a slight stamp. It is used to commence a number of figures.

4 *THE ATTACK*

Commence with Normal Hold. Precede with Sur Place.

	Man	**Lady**	**Timing**
	Facing LOD or diagonally wall, weight on LF	Backing LOD or diagonally wall, weight on RF	
1	Appel on RF	Appel on LF	1
2	LF forward	RF back	2
3	RF to side, turning ¼ turn to left between Steps 2 and 3	LF to side, turning ¼ turn to left	1
4	LF closes to RF	RF closes to LF	2

N.B. The Attack may also be danced without turn.

Follow with Sur Place.

5 *CHASSES TO RIGHT AND LEFT (WITH OR WITHOUT ELEVATION)*

A. Chasses to Right:

Commence in Normal Hold. Precede with Sur Place.

	Man	**Lady**	**Timing**
	Facing centre, weight on LF	Facing wall, weight on RF	
1	RF to side	LF to side	1
2	LF closes to RF	RF closes to LF	2
3	RF to side	LF to side	1
4	LF closes to RF	RF closes to LF	2

N.B. The Chasses to Right may be commenced in any direction and may be curved Right or Left. They may be repeated.

Follow with Sur Place.

B. Chasses to Left:

Commence in Normal Hold. Precede with Sur Place.

	Man	Lady	Timing
	Facing wall, weight on LF	Facing centre, weight on RF	
1	Appel on RF	Appel on LF	1
2	LF to side	RF to side	2
3	RF closes to LF	LF closes to RF	1
4	LF to side	RF to side	2

N.B. The Chasses to Left may be commenced in any direction and can be curved to Right or Left. They may be repeated.

Follow with Sur Place.

C. The Elevations:

The Elevations are Chasses to Right or Left, danced with a change of height, either high on the toes with legs straight, or with feet flat and knees slightly flexed

(*a*) 2 Chasses up, 2 Chasses down	1 2 1 2
	1 2 1 2
(*b*) 1 Chasse up, 1 Chasse down	1 2 1 2

6 *THE DRAG*

Commence in Normal Hold. Precede with Sur Place.

	Man	Lady	Timing
	Facing centre, weight on LF	Facing wall, weight on RF	
1–4	Dance 2 Chasses to right with Elevation	Dance 2 Chasses to left with Elevation	1 2 1 2
5–8	2 Chasses to right; down	2 Chasses to left; down	1 2 1 2
9–12	Repeat Steps 1–4	Repeat Steps 1–4	1 2 1 2
13	RF to side, long step; down; Ball flat, bending right knee	LF to side, long step; down; Ball flat, bending left knee	1
14–16	Drag LF to RF, taking weight on LF on step 16, straightening right knee	Drag RF to LF, taking weight on RF on step 16, straightening left knee	2 1 2

Follow with Sur Place.

7 *PROMENADE LINK*

Commence in Normal Hold. Precede with Sur Place.

	Man	Lady	Timing
	Facing LOD, weight on LF	Backing LOD, weight on RF	
1	Appel on RF	Appel on LF	1
2	LF to side in Promenade Position, heel flat, turning 1/8 to left between 1 and 2	RF to side in Promenade Position, heel flat, turning 1/8 to right between 1 and 2	2
3	RF forward and across in Promenade Position	LF forward in Promenade Position	1
4	LF closes to RF, turning 1/8 to left between 2 and 4	RF closes to LF, turning 3/8 to left between 3 and 4	2

N.B. This figure may be danced in other directions.

Follow with Chasses to Right or Sur Place.

8 *SEPARATION*

Commence in Normal Hold. Precede with Chasses to Right or Sur Place.

	Man	Lady	Timing
	Facing LOD, weight on LF	Backing LOD, weight on RF	
1	Appel on RF	Appel on LF	1
2	LF forward, commencing to lead Lady to move away	RF back	2
3	RF closes to LF, leading Lady to move away and releasing hold with right hand	LF back, releasing left hand	1
4	Sur Place on LF	RF closes to LF	2
5–8	4 Sur Place, RLRL, leading Lady forward to Normal Position and Hold	4 Basic Movements forward, LRLR	1 2 1 2

N.B. Steps 3–7 on balls of feet.

Elevation may be used on 4, gradually lowering over Steps 5–8. Follow with Sur Place or Chasses to Right.

9 *SEPARATION WITH LADY'S CAPING WALKS*

	Man	Lady	Timing
	Facing LOD, weight on LF	Backing LOD, weight on RF	
1–8	Commence in Normal Hold and precede this figure with the Separation, leading Lady forward to right side over Steps 5–8, raising left arm and Lady's right arm on 8.		1 2 1 2 1 2 1 2
9–16	Man stands still (or marks time) for the next 8 counts, leading Lady to pass from his right side to left side behind his back, to finish in front of him	(Lady walks forward	1 2 1 2 1 2 1 2 L R L R L R R)

Follow with Sur Place.

10 *HUIT (CAPE)*

Commence in Promenade Position, feet slightly apart. Precede with Sur Place, turning Lady to Promenade Position, or 1-4 of Ecart.

	Man		Lady	Timing
	Facing diagonally wall, weight on LF		Facing diagonally centre, weight on RF	
1	RF forward and across in Promenade Position		LF forward and across in Promenade Position	1
2	LF closes to RF, turning 1/8 to right between 1 and 2 to face wall		RF to side, turning left; ball of foot	2
3–8	Sur Place RLRLRL; ball flat on each step		Replace weight to LF, ball flat, ½ turn to left between 1 and 3	1
		4	RF forward and across	2
		5	LF to side, turning to right; ball of foot	1
		6	Replace weight to RF; ball flat; ½ turn to right between 4 and 6	2
		7	LF forward towards partner	1

Man	**Lady**	**Timing**
	8 RF closes to LF, 1/8 turn to left between 7 and 8	2

N.B. Man leads Lady to move to his left side on 2, to his right side on 5, towards him on 7 and to normal position on 8.

Follow with Sur Place or Chasses to Right.

11 *ECART (FALLAWAY WHISK) AND PROMENADE LINK TO RIGHT.*

Commence in Normal Hold. Precede with Sur Place.

	Man	**Lady**	**Timing**
	Facing wall, weight on LF	Backing wall, weight on RF	
1	Appel on RF	Appel on LF	1
2	LF forward	RF back	2
3	RF to side and slightly back in Fallaway; ball flat; turning 1/8 to left between 2 and 3	LF to side and slightly back in Fallaway; ball flat; turning 1/8 to right between 2 and 3	1
4	LF crosses behind RF in Fallaway; ball flat	RF crosses behind LF in Fallaway; ball flat	2
5	RF forward and across in Promenade Position	LF forward and across in Promenade Position	1
6	LF closes to RF, turning 1/8 to right to face wall	RF closes to LF, turning 1/8 to left to face centre	2
7	RF to side	LF to side	1
8	LF closes to RF	RF closes to LF	2

N.B. This figure may also be commenced facing diagonally wall or L OD

Follow with Chasses to Right.

AMALGAMATIONS

1 4 Sur Place; The Drag; 4 Sur Place.

2 4 Sur Place; Attack; 2 Chasses to Right; 4 Sur Place.

3 Sur Place; Promenade Link; 2 Chasses to Right; Sur Place.

4 4 Sur Place; Ecart and Promenade Link to Right; 2 Chasses to Right.

5 4 Sur Place; 1–4 of Ecart; Huit.
6 4 Sur Place; Promenade Link; 2 Chasses to Right, turning to face LOD; Separation; Sur Place.
7 8 Sur Place; Separation with Lady's Caping Walks; 8 Sur Place.

10

JIVE

INTRODUCTION

The Jive was brought to England from the United States by the GI's during the Second World War. It caused a great change in the English ballroom dancing scene. Because of the war, the atmosphere of 'live for today and let tomorrow look after itself' set a pattern for dancing with a gay, almost abandoned style. The dance developed on rather athletic lines and became 'Jitterbug', with lifts and exciting jumps. Because of this it was unsuitable and dangerous for the public ballroom and was banned except as a competition dance; it then went through many stages and became known by various names such as 'Lindy', 'West Coast Swing', 'American Swing', 'Rock and Roll', and probably more. Although each new title brought with it something slightly different, the same base was there: the man would turn the lady under his arm from left to right, sometimes spinning her, sometimes passing her behind his back, but mainly marking the rhythm and leading the lady to dance the shapes by turning and spinning.

The Jive was then groomed by dancing teachers and a dance emerged which could be taught and danced as a social or exhibition dance. The Rock and Roll was based on the same shapes but with an easier, less energetic timing. Both have a place and very often a good Jive dancer combines the two dances.

The Jive is a non-progressive dance and can be danced in a fairly small space when the floor is crowded.

This dance is a *must* for any social dancer, because, with the revival of the Big Band sound, the music is played many times during an average dance. (P.S.)

THE DANCE

Hold. This is similar to other Latin dances but easier and more relaxed, with the arms held slightly lower. The man must learn to get music 'in his hands' to give the correct lead to his girl, because most of the 'talking' is done with hands. The knees must have a slight, springy action, not a pronounced bounce, but must be very pliable to cope with the speed of the music.

Footwork. All steps are taken on the ball of the foot with the heel lightly lowering to the floor. Knees are naturally flexed. The individual steps are small.

Chasse. A group of three steps taken sideways to right or left, backwards or forwards, or turning to right or left. The chasse is counted 'Three *a* four' and is usually danced in sets of two: 'Three *a* four, three *a* four'. The feet do not close on the second step as this would make the steps rather too sharp.

It is advisable to practise the chasse to the left and to the right with the linking back step many, many times before attempting to put any of the other figures together.

Initial Exercise. The following exercise will help the beginner to feel the dance rhythm in the feet and hands before embarking on the actual step patterns that will eventually become his or her Jive. There are no real alignments although some are given as a guide to the beginner.

Commence facing wall, feet very slightly apart, weight on RF, hands held in front as though holding partner with both hands, keeping them slightly low and loose at the wrist. Dance three very small steps (Jive chasse) almost in place, travelling slightly to left and using hands to the same timing as though turning left in the car, left hand down. Now follow with three small steps almost in place, travelling slightly to right and turning hands to normal position. Step back with left foot, small step (Lady RF) with slight pulling action from hands, replace weight into RF in place and return hands to original position, so the little dance would go something like this: 1 2 3—4 5 6—back, step.

A very slight pause will be felt on Steps 3 and 6 with a positive change of weight on the 'back, step'. Try this exercise until the steps fit quite fast music and make sure to use the hands in time with the music.

This little exercise can then be turned to the left, making a ¼ turn each time; first sequence commences facing wall, second one facing Line of Dance, third one facing centre, fourth one facing against Line of Dance, fifth one facing wall, having returned to original position. This will help the man particularly to understand how the dance turns to the left, and the ¼ turn is the amount of turn he will normally make. The lady, of course, will turn more when she eventually turns under arm *etc.*

When practising this turn to left, the value of the left hand down on the first chasse will be felt to help the body to get a slight sway to the left as though turning a corner in a car or on a bicycle. The man will make his steps very, very small as he is on the inside of the circle, the lady slightly larger because she has the outside of the circle to follow. The ability to dance this exercise well will make the study and dancing of the rest of the figures in the Jive reasonably easy.

Figures Described

1. *Jive Chasse to L and R*
2. *Fallaway Rock*
3. *Fallaway Throwaway*
4. *Link Rock*
5. *Link and Whip*
6. *Change of Places Right to Left*
7. *Change of Places Left to Right*
8. *Change of Hands behind back*
9. *Left Shoulder 'Shove'*
10. *Walks in Promenade*
11. *Kick Ball Change*

1 *JIVE CHASSES TO LEFT AND RIGHT*

(*Man or Lady*)

Commence in Normal Hold *or* Double Hand Hold, Man facing wall, knees softly flexed.

	Chasse to left	**Timing**	**Chasse to right**	**Timing**
1	LF to side (small step)	3	RF to side (small step)	3
2	Close RF towards LF	a	Close LF towards RF	a
3	LF to side (small step)	4	RF to side (small step)	4
4	RF to side (small step)	3	LF to side (small step)	3
5	Close LF towards RF	a	Close RF towards LF	a
6	RF to side (small step)	4	LF to side (small step)	4

2 *FALLAWAY ROCK*

Commence in Normal Hold, weight on RF, facing wall. Precede with Chasse to Right (RLR)

	Man	**Timing**	**Lady**	**Timing**
1	LF back in Fallaway tnrning $\frac{1}{8}$ to left turning Lady to R	1	RF back in Fallaway turning $\frac{1}{8}$ to right	1
2	Replace weight forward to RF in Promenade Position commencing to turn Lady to L	2	Replace weight forward to LF in Promenade Position	2
3–5	LF to side to Chasse LRL turning R to face wall	3a4	RF to side to Chasse RLR turning L to face centre	3a4
6–8	RF to side to Chasse RLR	3a4	LF to side to Chasse LRL	3a4

End in Closed Facing Position. Follow with Change of Places Right to Left *or* Fallaway Throwaway.

3 *FALLAWAY THROWAWAY*

Commence in normal hold, weight on RF, facing wall.

	Man	Timing	Lady	Timing
1–5	1–5 of Fallaway Rock (LRLRL). On Step 5 lower joined hands and lean slightly to L	1 2 3a4	1–5 of Fallaway Rock (RLRLR). Lean slightly to R on Step 5	1 2 3a4
6–8	RF forward to Chasse RLR turning L to face LOD, leading Lady to move away and releasing hold with R hand	3a4	LF back to Chasse LRL turning L to back LOD	3a4

End in Open Facing Position. Follow with Link Rock *or* Change of Places Left to Right.

4 *LINK ROCK*

Commence in Open Facing Position, weight on RF, direction according to preceding figure.

	Man	Timing	Lady	Timing
1	LF back	1	RF back	1
2	Replace weight forward to RF	2	Replace weight forward to LF	2
3–5	LF forward to Chasse LRL leading Lady forward	3a4	RF forward to Chasse RLR	3a4
6–8	RF to side to Chasse RLR regaining normal hold	3a4	LF to side Chasse LRL regaining normal hold	3a4

End in Closed Facing Position. Follow with Fallaway Rock.

5 *LINK AND WHIP*

Commence in Open Facing Position, weight on RF. Direction according to preceding figure.

	Man	Timing	Lady	Timing
1	LF back	1	RF back	1
2	Replace weight forward to RF	2	Replace weight forward to LF	2
3–5	LF forward to Chasse LRL to end LF diagonally forward, having led Lady forward, regaining normal hold	3a4	RF forward to Chasse RLR to end with RF forward between partner's feet, regaining normal hold	3a4
6	RF crosses behind LF commencing to turn R	1	LF forward towards Man's R side, turning R	1
7	LF to side (small step) continuing to turn R	2	RF forward between partner's feet, small step	2
8–10	RF to side, very small step, to Chasse RLR completing required amount of turn to end in Fallaway position	3a4	LF to side to Chasse LRL continuing to turn R, ending in Fallaway position	3a4

End in Fallaway position. Follow with Change of Places R to L *or* Walks in Promenade Position.

N.B. Up to a complete turn can be made.

6 *CHANGE OF PLACES RIGHT TO LEFT*

Commence in Normal Hold, weight on RF, facing wall

	Man	Timing	Lady	Timing
1–5	1–5 of Fallaway Rock LRLRL. On Step 5 raise joined hands and commence to turn Lady to her R	1 2 3a4	1–5 of Fallaway Rock RLRLR. On Step 5 commence to turn to R	1 2 3a4

	Man	Timing	Lady	Timing
6–8	RF forward to Chasse RLR turning L to face LOD leading Lady to complete her turn to R under the raised arms, having released hold with R hand. Lower joined hands at end of Lady's turn	3a4	Continue to turn to R under the raised arms and Chasse LRL to end LF back, backing LOD	3a4

End in Open Position. Follow with the Change of Places from Left to Right or Link Rock.

7 *CHANGE OF PLACES LEFT TO RIGHT*

Commence in Open Facing Position, weight on RF, facing LOD having danced Change of Places Right to Left.

	Man	Timing	Lady	Timing
1–2	1–2 of Link (LR)	1 2	1–2 of Link (RL)	1 2
3–5	Almost close LF to RF to Chasse LRL turning to R to face wall and leading Lady to turn to her L under the raised arms	3a4	Chasse RLR turning to L under the raised arms	3a4
6–8	RF forward to Chasse RLR leading Lady to complete her turn to L and lowering the joined hands at end of Lady's turn	3a4	Continuing to turn L, LF back to Chasse LRL to end backing wall	3a4

End in Open Facing Position. Follow with Link Rock.

8 *CHANGE OF HANDS BEHIND BACK*

Commence in Open Facing Position, Man facing wall, having danced Change of Places Left to Right

	Man	Timing	Lady	Timing
1–2	1–2 of Link (LR)	1 2	1–2 of Link (RL)	1 2
3–5	Placing R hand over Lady's R hand and releasing hold with L hand, LF forward to Chasse LRL leading Lady forward to R side	3a4	RF forward to Chasse RLR moving to man's R side and commencing to turn to R	3a4
6–8	Changing Lady's R hand into Man's L behind his back, Chasse turning to L to face centre, RLR to end RF back	3a4	Chasse turning to R to face wall LRL to end LF back	3a4

N.B. The Man may place Lady's R hand on his waist on Step 3, releasing hold with R hand and allowing the Lady's R hand to trail around his waist, then catching it in his L hand again at the completion of his turn.

End in Open Facing Position. Follow with Link Rock.

9 *LEFT SHOULDER 'SHOVE'*

Commence in L Side-by-Side Position, having danced Fallaway Throwaway, turning to end with partner on L side, facing wall.

	Man	Timing	Lady	Timing
1	LF back	1	RF back	1
2	Replace weight forward to RF	2	Replace weight to LF	2
3–5	LF to side to Chasse LRL. Move towards each other with shoulders touching	3a4	RF to side to Chasse RLR. Move towards each other with shoulders touching	3a4

	Man	Timing	Lady	Timing
6–8	Giving Lady a slight push with L shoulder, RF to side to Chasse RLR. Move slightly away from each other	3a4	LF to side to Chasse LRL. Move slightly away from each other	3a4

End in Left Side-by-Side Position facing wall and continue into Link Rock turning to face partner on first step.

10 *WALKS IN PROMENADE*

Commence in Normal Hold, man facing wall.

	Man	Timing	Lady	Timing
1–2	1–2 of Fallaway Rock (LR)	1 2	1–2 of Fallaway Rock (RL)	1 2
3–5	LF diag. forward to Chasse LRL turning Lady to L	3a4	RF to side to Chasse RLR turning to L	3a4
6–8	RF forward and across in Promenade Position to Chasse RLR turning Lady to R		LF forward in Promenade Position to Chasse LRL turning to R	3a4

Steps 3–8 may be repeated. End in Promenade Position—continue into Steps 3 to 8 of Change of Places Right to Left.

An alternative method of dancing the Walks is to substitute single steps for the Chasses *i.e.* LRLR QQQQ.

11 *KICK BALL CHANGE*

Commence having danced Change of Places Right to Left. This action is used in place of 1–2 of the Link.

	Man	Timing	Lady	Timing
1	Flick LF forward	1	Flick RF forward	1
2	Place LF slightly back, approx toe of LF to heel of RF (Ball of foot)	a	Place RF slightly back, approx toe of RF to heel of LF (Ball of foot)	a
3	Replace weight on to RF in place	2	Replace weight on to LF in place	2

N.B. This could be danced in Promenade Position.

SUGGESTED AMALGAMATIONS

A Jive Chasses to L and R
Fallaway Rock
Fallaway Throwaway
Link Rock

B Fallaway Rock
Change of Places R to L
Link Rock

C Fallaway Rock
Change of Places R to L
Change of Places L to R
Link and Whip

D Fallaway Throwaway to L Side-by-Side Position
Left Shoulder 'Shove'
Change of Hands behind Back
Link and Whip

E Jive Chasses to Left and Right
Fallaway Rock
Walks in Promenade Position
Kick Ball Change in Promenade Position (LF Man) (RF Lady). Repeat the Kick Ball Change
5–8 of Fallaway Throwaway
Link Rock

Note: The Jive Chasses to L and R are only used to start the dance as for practice.

11

ROCK AND ROLL

All the figures described for the Jive can be danced in Rock and Roll rhythm. The difference in the two styles is the rather more relaxed, *lazy* and carefree character of the Rock and Roll compared to the more energetic Jive; the timing of the steps also varies and whereas Rock and Roll often develops as a 'personal' dance with the Man often making up his own style and steps which can sometimes be quite difficult to follow, the Jive remains fairly consistent and can usually be followed by the girl if she has studied the basic theme and rhythm.

The Rock and Roll is often described as the lazy man's Jive because the Jiver will mark three steps on each Chasse action and the Rock and Roller will only mark one.

The following exercise will help the dancer to understand the feeling of the rhythm in relation to the step pattern.

Step 1	Commence facing the wall, weight on RF, taking a small step to side on LF with only part weight on the foot	*Count* 1
	Then put the full weight on to the step	,, '*and*'
	(Now you are standing on your LF)	
Step 2	Place part weight on to your RF	,, 2
	Then put full weight on to the RF	,, '*and*'
	(Now you are standing on your RF having danced two steps)	
Step 3	Now take a small step back with your LF and stand on it	,, 3

Step 4 Place the weight onto your RF in place *Count* 4

Repeat the four steps starting with your LF and the count will go:

1 *and* 2 *and* 3 4, 1 *and* 2 *and* 3 4

The following analysis gives various ways of timing the steps listed in the Jive Section, once you have mastered the basic idea.

All the figures listed in Jive may be danced in Rock rhythm by using 'Tap, step' or just one 'step' (LF to side without weight, then with weight) instead of a Chasse—the beat value is the same; for instance the Fallaway Rock timing would be:

Method 1 (as described with Chasses)

Steps	L	R	L	R	L	R	L	R	
Count	1	2	3	a	4	3	a	4	$= 1\frac{1}{2}$ bars

Method 2 (using 'tap step' in place of Chasses)

Steps	L	R	L	L	R	R	
Count	Q	Q	Q	Q	Q	Q	$= 1\frac{1}{2}$ bars

Method 3 (using a single step in place of Chasse)

Steps	L	R	L	R	
Count	Q	Q	S	S	$= 1\frac{1}{2}$ bars

The Lady will always dance the normal opposite.

12

CHA CHA CHA

INTRODUCTION

The Cha Cha Cha is perhaps the most popular of the Latin dances. The name rolls off the tongue, and the rhythm is easy to understand. The dance almost speaks for itself through the music where the beat of the Bongo Drums and the Marracas seem to say 'Cha, Cha Cha, Step, Step'.

The dance originally came from Cuba and its forerunner is the Mambo, which is fast and more for the specialist. This developed into the Triple Mambo (hence the 3 counts) but gradually a slower, more pronounced and clearer interpretation of the rhythm was evolved, called the Cha Cha Cha (sometimes referred to as the Cha Cha). Music arrangers seemed able to adapt many popular melodies to the Cha Cha Cha rhythm, thus creating continuous interest in the dance. (P.S.)

THE DANCE

Music. Take care to buy records that are written as Cha Cha Chas, and if possible begin with a slow one. When a dancer is efficient he can begin the dance with the Cha Cha Cha Chasse, or with the forward step on the left foot. Some dancers even prefer to commence with the backward half of the Basic Movement. There is no set rule about this. Because of its Latin parentage the rhythm is felt in the hips more than in the feet, although of course it is essential to learn the foot positions first. It is not necessary to have a large repertoire of figures because the feeling of the music is satisfaction in itself. Five or six figures would be more than enough, and with practice these can be changed around to make interesting and challenging patterns, always remembering, of course, the art of leading or following your partner into the change of figures. Tempo: 30 to 34 bars to the minute.

Footwork and Hold. As in the Jive and Rock, the man plays a leading and supporting role and in many advanced figures the girl has the more active part of the dance, turning under arm and moving away from and towards her partner. The steps should be small and rhythmic with the emphasis on the hips and body rhythm as in all Latin dances. Rhythm is the essence of the dance. The hold is similar to the Rumba and Samba, just slightly apart from partner, and some figures are danced without hold, such as the Time Steps. The footwork is ball flat throughout, and when stepping backwards the heel will lower later than when stepping forward, in order to avoid the weight dropping backwards. Good poise, balance and strong positive leg and foot action are essential to achieve the feeling of the Cha Cha Cha.

How to learn the dance. First work on the Cha Cha Cha Chasses to right and to left. Mark out the three steps keeping each step small, and give slightly more time to the third step; feel quite a positive pause, in fact to count 'Cha Cha Pause' is a very good way to rehearse. When the feeling of the two Chasses has been achieved, then practise the two steps that link the Chasses together, making sure that each step is a positive foot and weight change, like marking time. Then put the first five steps into one unit, first making sure that you have five positive steps in the first half, and five positive steps in the second half. Having achieved this continue to *practise* the 10 steps that make the basic pattern, because this Basic Movement is the foundation upon which all the other step patterns are built.

Figures Described

1 *RF AND LF CHA CHA CHA CHASSE*

Right foot Cha Cha Cha Chasse: commence feet apart.

	Man	Timing	Lady	Timing
1	Small step to side RF	4	Small step to side LF	4
2	Move LF slightly towards RF	&	Move RF slightly towards LF	&
3	Very small step to side RF	1	Very small step to side LF	1

Left foot Cha Cha Cha Chasse: Commence feet apart.

	Man	Timing	Lady	Timing
1	Small step to side LF	4	Small step to side RF	4
2	Move RF slightly towards LF	&	Move LF slightly towards RF	&
3	Very small step to side LF	1	Very small step to side RF	1

2 *BASIC MOVEMENT IN PLACE*

Commence feet apart. For practice face wall.

	Man	Timing	Lady	Timing
1	Step on LF in place	2	Step on RF in place	2
2	Step on RF in place	3	Step on LF in place	3
3–5	Dance a LF Chasse	4&1	Dance a RF Chasse	4&1
6	Step on RF in place	2	Step on LF in place	2
7	Step on LF in place	3	Step on RF in place	3
8–10	Dance a RF Chasse	4&1	Dance a LF Chasse	4&1

3 *THE BASIC MOVEMENT*

Commence in normal hold, feet apart, weight on RF facing wall. Figure turns gradually left.

	Man	Timing	Lady	Timing
1	LF forward commencing to turn to L	2	RF back commencing to turn L	2
2	Replace weight to RF continuing to turn	3	Replace weight to LF continuing to turn	3
3–5	LF to side and slightly back to Chasse LRL continuing turning to L	4&1	RF to side to Chasse RLR, continuing turning to L	4&1
6	RF back continuing to turn L	2	LF forward continuing to turn L	2
7	Replace weight to LF continuing to turn	3	Replace weight to RF continuing to turn	3
8–10	RF to side to Chasse RLR continuing to turn L to face centre	4&1	LF to side and slightly back to Chasse LRL continuing to turn L to back centre	4&1

N.B. The Basic Movement may be danced with or without turn to Left.

End in normal hold. Finish in direction required for next figure *i.e.* if New York is next figure, end facing wall.

4 *NEW YORK*

Commence in normal hold, feet apart, weight on RF, facing wall. Precede with the Basic Movement, releasing hold with R hand ready to step into L Side-by-Side Position.

	Man	Timing	Lady	Timing
1	Turning to R, LF forward in L Side-by-Side position, facing against LOD	2	Turning to L, RF forward in L Side-by-Side position, facing against LOD	2
2	Replace weight to RF commencing to turn to L	3	Replace weight to LF commencing to turn to R	3
3–5	LF to side to Chasse LRL turning L to face wall and Lady, releasing hold with L hand and taking Lady's L hand in R hand	4&1	RF to side to Chasse RLR turning R to face centre and Man	4&1

	Man	Timing	Lady	Timing
6	Turning to L, RF forward in R Side-by-Side position, facing LOD	2	LF forward in R Side-by-Side position, facing LOD	2
7	Replace weight to LF commencing to turn to R	3	Replace weight to RF commencing to turn to L	3
8–10	RF to side to Chasse RLR turning R to face wall and Lady, releasing hold with R hand and taking Lady's R hand in L hand	4&1	LF to side to Chasse LRL turning L to face centre and Man	4&1

Follow with a Spot Turn (Man turning R and Lady L) or a Basic Movement *or* repeat Steps 1–5 and follow with a Spot Turn (Man turning L and Lady R).

5 *TIME STEPS*

Commence in Normal or Open Facing Position with or without hold, feet apart, weight on RF or LF and commencing direction according to amalgamation.

	Man	Timing	Lady	Timing
	LF Time Step			
1	LF behind RF toe slightly turned out	2	RF behind LF	2
2	Replace weight to RF	3	Replace weight to LF	3
3–5	LF to side to Chasse LRL	4&1	RF to side Chasse RLR	4&1
	RF Time Step			
1	RF behind LF toe slightly turned out	2	LF behind RF	2
2	Replace weight to LF	3	Replace weight to RF	3
3–5	RF to side to Chasse RLR	4&1	LF to side to Chasse LRL	4&1

N.B. For precedes and follows see Amalgamations.

6 *SHOULDER TO SHOULDER*

Commence in normal hold (or without hold), weight on RF slightly forward. Precede with Spot Turn or Basic Movement preparing to step outside partner on her L side.

	Man	Timing	Lady	Timing
1	LF forward outside partner on L side	2	RF back	2
2	Replace weight to RF	3	Replace weight to LF	3
3–5	LF to side to Chasse LRL turning ¼ to L	4&1	RF to side to Chàsse RLR turning ¼ to L	4&1
6	RF forward outside partner on R side	2	LF back	2
7	Replace weight to LF	3	Replace weight to RF	3
8–10	RF to side to Chasse RLR turning ¼ to R	4&1	LF to side to Chasse LRL turning ¼ to R	4&1

Repeat Steps 1–5 to end in Promenade Position and follow with a Spot Turn (Man turning to L and Lady to R) *or* Repeat Steps 1–10 to end in Closed Facing Position.

7 *SIDE BASIC*

Commence facing partner with or without hold, weight on RF. Precede with Basic Movement or 1–5 of New York into Steps 6–10 of Side Basic.

	Man	Timing	Lady	Timing
1	LF to side	2	RF to side	2
2	RF closes to LF	3	LF closes to RF	3
3	LF to side	4	RF to side	4
4	RF closes towards LF	a	LF closes towards RF	a
5	LF to side	1	RF to side	1
6	RF closes to LF	2	LF closes to RF	2
7	LF to side	3	RF to side	3
8	RF closes towards LF	4	LF closes towards RF	4
9	LF to side	a	RF to side	a
10	RF closes to LF	1	LF closes to RF	1

8 *THE THREE CHA CHA CHAS*

These are 3 Cha Cha Cha Chasses danced forward, backward or forward side-by-side, counted 4 and 1, 2 and 3, 4 and 1.

In Right Side-by-Side Position: After 2 or 12 of Hand to Hand, 3 Forward Chasses for Man and Lady.
No turn, or turn slightly towards partner on the first and third Chasses and slightly away on the second Chasse.
Follow with Spot Turn to Left (Lady to Right).

9 *SPOT TURNS*

These are usually danced individually, but may be danced together, in which case Man dances a Left turn while Lady dances a Right turn, or vice versa.

	Spot Turn to Right, Man or Lady	**Timing**	**Spot Turn to Left, Man or Lady**	**Timing**
1	LF forward turning to R making approx $\frac{3}{8}$ turn to R	2	RF forward turning to L making approx $\frac{3}{8}$ turn to L	2
2	RF forward continuing to turn approx $\frac{3}{8}$	3	LF forward continuing to turn approx $\frac{3}{8}$	3
3–5	Still turning approx $\frac{1}{4}$ to R Chasse sideways LRL Amount of Turn: 1 complete turn End facing partner	4&1	Still turning approx $\frac{1}{4}$ to L Chasse sideways RLR Amount of Turn: 1 complete turn End facing partner	4&1

10 *ALEMANA TURN*

(Lady's under arm turn to R). Commence in Normal Hold, feet apart. Precede with Basic Movement.

	Man	**Timing**	**Lady**	**Timing**
1	LF forward	2	RF back	2
2	Replace weight on to RF	3	Replace weight on to LF	3
3–5	Cha Cha Cha Chasse in place (LRL)	4&1	Cha Cha Cha Chasse (RLR) to side commencing to turn to R	4&1
6	RF back leading Lady to turn to R under L arm releasing hold with R hand	2	LF forward still turning	2
7	Replace weight on to LF	3	RF forward still turning	3
8–10	Cha Cha Cha Chasse to side. Regain normal hold	4&1	Still turning to R Cha Cha Cha Chasse (LRL) to side to end facing partner. Regain normal hold	4&1

Follow with Basic Movement or Hand to Hand.

11 *HAND TO HAND*

Commence in Normal Facing Position in Double Hold, feet apart, Man facing wall. Precede with Alemana Turn.

	Man	**Timing**	**Lady**	**Timing**
1	Turning to L, LF back in R Side-by-Side position, backing against LOD releasing hold with L hand	2	Turning ¼ to R, RF back in R Side-by-Side position releasing hold with R hand	2
2	Replace weight on RF commencing to turn to R	3	Replace weight on to LF commencing to turn L	3
3–5	LF to side to Chasse LRL turning R to face wall and Lady and taking double hold	4&1	RF to side to Chasse RLR turning to L to face centre and partner	4&1
6	Turning to R and releasing hold with R hand, RF back in L Side-by-Side position, backing LOD	2	Turning ¼ to L, LF back in L Side-by-Side position	2

	Man	**Timing**	**Lady**	**Timing**
7	Replace weight on LF commencing to turn L	3	Replace weight on RF commencing to turn R	3
8–10	RF to side to Chasse RLR turning L to face wall and Lady taking double hold in Closed Facing Position	4&1	LF to side to Chasse LRL	4&1

Repeat Steps 1–10 or follow with Basic Movement.
Repeat Steps 1–5 and follow with a Spot Turn (Man turning to L and Lady to R).

12 *FORWARD AND BACK RUN*

Commence in Normal Hold. Precede with the Basic Movement. This can be used by Lady and Man dancing normal opposite or is great fun when Man moves back away from Lady and she moves back away from Man and then both return and continue into New York or Basic Movement.

	Man	**Timing**	**Lady**	**Timing**
1	LF forward	2	RF back	2
2	Replace weight to RF	3	Replace weight to LF	3
3–5	Three small steps travelling back, passing feet, LRL	4&1	Three small steps travelling forward, passing feet, RLR	4&1

N.B. Steps 1 and 2 are almost in place.

6	RF back	2	LF forward	2
7	Replace weight to LF	3	Replace weight to RF	3
8–10	Three small steps travelling forward, passing feet, RLR	4&1	Three small steps travelling back, passing feet, LRL	4&1

N.B. Steps 1,2,6 and 7 are almost in place.

SUGGESTED AMALGAMATIONS

A Basic Movement (repeated)
New York, then repeat 1–5
Spot Turn to L for Man
Spot Turn to R for Lady
Continue into Basic Movement

B Basic Movement (repeated)
Alemana Turn
Two Time Steps
Continue into Basic Movement

C Basic Movement
Alemana Turn
Hand to Hand. Repeat Steps 1–5
Spot Turn to L for Man
(Spot Turn to R for Lady)

D Basic Movement
New York
Side Basic
Back Run (Both travelling back)
Forward Run (Both travelling forward)
New York. Repeat 1–5
Spot Turn to L for Man
(Spot Turn to R for Lady)
Continue into Basic Movement

E Alemana Turn to end with Double Hand Hold
Hand to Hand. Repeat Steps 1 and 2
Three Cha Cha Cha Chasses forward in R Side-by-Side Position
Spot Turn to L for Man
(Spot Turn to R for Lady)
Continue with Basic Movement

13

SOLO DANCING—DISCO STYLE

INTRODUCTION

Beat and Disco style dancing can be likened to the rhythmic movement danced by the natives of Africa in which people expressed, in dance form, their feelings of happiness, sorrow, hate, and even war, to their own music provided by instruments made from the bark of trees, animal skins, tuberous plants, *etc.* In this form of dance one does not need a partner and the personal interpretation of the music usually reflects the mood of the dancer. However, a few basic movements are a great help, and a study of the basic Disco steps will give the dancer a start, then the body movement and arm and hip actions can be added. Arm movements often reflect day to day actions, such as serving at tennis, skating, swimming, answering the telephone, *etc.*

There is a tremendous feeling of rhythmic exhilaration in being able to dance completely freely, uninhibited and unencumbered by a partner. However, this form of dance is anti-social and should only be a small part, not a whole evening's dance programme. Nevertheless many discotheques play only this type of music, often very loud, so if you visit this type of dancing venue, you must equip yourself with the general style of dancing. Dancing Schools usually cover what are known as 'Line Dances' where the pupils are taught a small sequence, usually to 4, 6 or 8 bars of music. The steps are Disco steps but in a set sequence to a particular record. This is a very relaxed way to learn rhythm and feeling to music, similar to limbering in Jazz or Classical Ballet. Many of the actual foot patterns taught are taken from dances like the Samba, Cha Cha Cha and Jive, and so help to guide the dancer into the natural feeling for these figures. A line dance can often be adapted to a 'facing partner' dance by changing the step so that the couple are dancing on opposite feet, and not on the same foot as each other. (P.S.)

THE DANCE MUSIC

Pop music changes from month to month. The music writers, Pop groups and musicians are continually composing new types of music and new combinations of sound, and the dancing teachers try to interpret this music in dance form. These trends may only last a short time but are fun while they last.

Footwork. The first and most important part of Beat dancing is to develop rhythmic feeling in the legs and body before attempting steps. Work on the following exercises—often called 'Popcorn'—and practise them to music.

INITIAL EXERCISE

Commence with feet together, your knees softly flexed (not bent); bounce your knees down and up, without moving your feet and counting 'One, two, one, two' (*single beat action*). Then gradually introduce a double bounce by counting '*a* one, *a* two, *a* one, *a* two'.

Allow the arms to swing softly, relax your shoulders and gradually let the body turn right and left as the knees bounce, without moving your feet. After rehearsing this to music for some time, gradually bring the right arm almost to the right ear in rhythm as though answering the telephone and then as the arm swings down lift up the left arm. This can be done to produce the effect of serving at tennis, milking a cow and so on, but must be in rhythm, using the knees continuously to the music. All parts of the body should feel relaxed and ready to be used to music at any time; for instance, a slight shoulder shake or an arm action might be part of a step and that part of the body must be ready. Part of the beat dance can be done in this way by using rhythmic arm and body movements and not foot movements. However, it is exhilarating to have some step patterns as well, so here are some simple ones that can be used in any order. Most Disco dancers develop just two or three foot patterns and alternate and repeat these according to the feeling of the music.

Disco can be danced as a 'solo' dance or in a circle type pattern with a number of friends all doing their 'own thing'.

	Man and lady	**Timing**
	Commence with weight on RF (direction not important)	
1	Step on to LF in place, bouncing knees down	a 1
2	Point RF forward and slightly to R on heel or toe, without weight, using slight body turn to R and allowing arms to swing into a soft shape with body. Knees will slightly straighten	a 2
3	Almost close RF to LF bouncing knees down	a 1
4	Point LF forward and slightly to L on heel or toe, without weight, using slight body turn to L allowing arms to swing into a soft shape with body. Knees will slightly straighten	a 2

Repeat this over and over again. An easy way to master the knee action is to say '*bend*' on the closing step and '*straight*' on the pointing step and sing it in rhythm—'*bend, straight, bend, straight*', *etc.*

Some dancers prefer to commence with the '*straight*' action as the feet close and the '*bend*' as the foot is pointed, but this is a personal thing which can develop when the dancer knows the basic step.

2 *SIDE BASIC*

		Timing
1	LF to side small step	a 1
2	Close RF to LF without weight with slight body turn to R	a 2
3	RF side small step. Return body to starting position.	a 1
4	Close LF to RF without weight, with slight body turn to L	a 2

N.B. The closing step without weight will end with the heel of the LF (or RF) approximately to the instep of the supporting foot with the toe turned out.

The arms can be used by turning the elbows in towards the body on the 'a 2' count and raising the hands slightly, but keep the action low and subtle.

3 *BEAT CHASSE*

		Timing
1	LF to side (small step)	a 1
2	RF almost closes to LF	a 2
3	LF to side small step	a 3
4	Close RF to LF without weight, with slight body turn to R	a 4

N.B. The closing step should be danced as in the Side Basic and the arms can be used in the same way.

Repeat these four steps starting with RF turning body slightly L on fourth Step.

The three step patterns described can be used in any order and each are repeated as often as desired. The joy of beat is the feeling of being able to change step when *you* feel like it.

The following are three 'Line' dances which are a disciplined form of disco dancing—several people dancing the same routine at the same time. This can be great fun at a party or dance.

THE SLOSH

This is the easiest and most popular 'Line' disco dance for beginners. It is danced in lines—Man and Lady using the same foot.

Music. Medium tempo strong beat Pop.
Commence facing the wall with weight on RF.

		Timing
Fig. 1	*Step*	
	1 LF to side	1
	2 RF closes, or almost closes, to LF	2
	3 LF to side	3
	4 Kick RF across LF	4
	(*Say '1 2 3 Kick'*)	
Fig. 2	Repeat *Fig. 1* to Right, starting with RF (Say '*1 2 3 Kick*')	1 2 3 4
Fig. 3	Repeat *Fig. 1* (Say '*1 2 3 Kick*')	1 2 3 4
Fig. 4	Repeat *Fig. 2* but kick LF up *behind* RF and touch L heel with R hand (Say '*1 2 3* Kick')	1 2 3 4
Fig. 5	Commencing to turn to R	
	Place LF down with weight	1
	Lift RF off floor in front, bending knee and slapping R knee with R hand	2
	Place RF down with weight	3
	Lift LF off floor in front with knee high and clap hands under L knee	4
	(Say '*step—lift—step—clap*')	
	Make a ¼ turn to right on the four steps.	
	Commence dance again from this new alignment.	

Repeat each sequence on a new line having made ¼ turn to R on each one.

THE SPLIT

A 'Line' dance to slow or reggae-type Beat music. Commence in lines, weight on RF.

		Timing
Fig. 1	LF to side	1
	Almost close RF to LF	2
	LF to side	3
	Tap RF to LF without weight	4
	(*Side—close—side Tap*)	
Fig. 2	Repeat these four steps starting with RF but when tapping LF to RF bend knees ready for jump action (*Side—close—side Tap*)	1 2 3 4

		Timing
Fig. 3	(*Split*) With a light jumping action split feet apart then bring them together with LF crossed in front of RF	1 2
Fig. 4	Keeping knees together rock on to RF in place and then on to LF in place. Finish with weight on LF	3 4
Fig. 5	Kick RF forward	1
	Cross RF in front of LF and turn a ¼ to the L	2
	Place LF to side small step	3
	Close RF to LF	4
	Repeat this dance from the beginning on new alignment.	

A little energetic but great fun. Music needs to be slightly slower than normal beat—the Reggae-type Beat music is ideal.

HOT ROCK

Can be used as a 'Line' dance or facing partner. When danced facing partner normal opposite foot is used.

Music: Good medium tempo strong Beat Pop.

Man: Commence facing partner, weight on LF.

		Timing
Fig. 1	Point RF to R side without weight	1
	Close RF to LF without weight	2
	Point RF to R side without weight	3
	Close RF to LF *with* weight	4
	Repeat these four steps starting with LF pointing to side	1 2 3 4
Fig. 2	As Fig. 1, but point RF slightly back instead of to side and look towards it	1 2 3 4
	Repeat these four steps but starting with LF pointing slightly back	1 2 3 4
Fig. 3	Lift RF off floor in front with knee high and touch knee with left elbow	1
	Place RF down without weight	2
	Lift RF off floor again and touch knee with left elbow	3
	Place RF down *with* weight	4
	Now repeat these four steps lifting LF off floor and touching knee with R elbow	1 2 3 4

		Timing
Fig. 4	Turn a $\frac{1}{4}$ to R then RF forward	1
	LF closes towards R	2
	RF forward and at end of step turn a $\frac{1}{2}$ to L	3
	Draw LF towards RF without weight, toe turned out	4
	(This figure can be likened to a skating action)	
	Repeat these four steps starting with LF making no turn on first step—end ready to start dance again.	1 2 3 4

Chant in rhythm:—*Point 2 3 4*
Point 2 3 4
Back 2 3 4
Back 2 3 4
Lift 2 3 4
Lift 2 3 4
Skate 2 3 4
Skate 2 3 4
Start again.

This dance is fun at parties if danced in a circle—in which case all are on same foot.

14

BOSSA NOVA

INTRODUCTION

This is a new dance but not really a new rhythm. The Bossa Nova is sometimes referred to as a jazzy Samba and the change in interpretation of the music brought about the dance. It has taken a long time to become popular, perhaps because the rhythm sounds rather 'busy' to the dancer and a little difficult to understand. (P.S.)

Music. Use authentic Bossa Nova music or follow the current trend in the dance, which is to use Baion music—a type of slow Samba.

Many 'pop' records, especially the backing orchestras of Pop stars, have a strong Bossa Nova or Baion beat and the steps described fit the feeling of this music, which has a strong 'Slow Quick Quick' rhythm.

Footwork, Hold and Action. Hold is as in Rumba. The dance is felt in the hips whereas the Samba is felt in the knees. Thus, use a strong hip action, similar to Rumba, not a knee bounce. Steps must be kept small.

Figures Described. The figures listed form an ideal routine and the dancer will find it a most satisfying dance.

1 *Side Basic*
2 *Forward and Back Basic*
3 *Cross Basic (Whisk)*
4 *Solo Turn*
5 *Push Away*
6 *Face to Face and Back to Back*

1 *SIDE BASIC*

Commence in normal Latin hold, or dance without hold.

	Man	Lady	Timing
1	Side LF dragging RF slightly towards LF	Side RF dragging LF slightly towards RF	S
2	Close RF to LF	Close LF to RF	Q
3	Replace weight on LF	Replace weight on RF	Q
	Repeat commencing with other foot		SQQ
	Repeat for the total of 4 bars.		SQQ SQQ

2 *FORWARD AND BACK BASIC*

	Man	Lady	Timing
1	Forward LF leaving RF in place	Back RF	S
2	Close RF to LF	Close LF to RF	Q
3	Replace weight on LF	Replace weight on RF	Q
4	Back RF leaving LF in place	Forward LF	S
	Close LF to RF	Close RF to LF	Q
6	Replace weight on RF in place	Replace weight on LF in place	Q
	Repeat for the total of 4 bars.		SQQ SQQ

3 *CROSS BASIC*

	Man	Lady	Timing
1	Side LF leaving RF in place	Side RF	S
2	Cross RF behind LF	Cross LF behind RF	Q
3	Replace weight on LF	Replace weight on RF	Q
4	Side RF leaving LF in place	Side LF	S
5	Cross LF behind RF	Cross RF behind LF	Q
6	Replace weight on RF	Replace weight on LF	Q
	Repeat for the total of 4 bars.		SQQ SQQ

4 *SOLO TURN—SIDE BASIC*

	Man	Lady	Timing
1	LF to side in Promenade Position commencing to turn to L	RF to side in Promenade Position commencing to turn to R	S
2	Forward RF in Promenade Position continuing to turn to L	Forward LF, turning R	Q
3	Replace weight forward to LF continuing to turn to L	Weight forward to RF, turning R	Q
4	Side RF, still turning L	Side LF, still turning R	S
5	Close LF to RF, facing partner	Close RF to LF, facing partner	Q
6	Mark time on RF in place to end facing partner	Mark time on LF	Q
	Repeat for the total of 4 bars.		SQQ SQQ

5 *PUSH AWAY*

	Man	Lady	Timing
1	LF back leaving RF in place at the same time 'pushing' Lady away with L hand. Release hold with R hand	RF back	S
2	Close RF to LF	Close LF to RF	Q
3	Replace weight to LF	Replace weight to RF	Q
4	RF forward leaving LF in place	LF forward	S
5	Close LF to RF, regaining normal hold	Close RF to LF	Q
6	Replace weight to RF	Replace weight to LF	Q
	Repeat for a total of 4 bars.		

6 *FACE TO FACE AND BACK TO BACK*

	Man	Lady	Timing
1	LF forward, turning to L and commencing to back partner, releasing hold	RF forward, turning to R	S
2	RF to side, small step, still turning L to almost back partner	LF to side, small step, still turning	Q
3	Close LF to RF, having completed ½ turn to L. Now backing partner	Close RF to LF, having completed ½ turn to R to back partner	Q
4	RF forward, turning to R and commencing to face partner	LF forward, turning to L	S
5	LF to side, small step, still turning R to almost face partner	RF to side, small step, still turning L	Q
6	Close RF to LF, having completed ½ turn to R. Now facing partner	Close LF to RF having completed ½ turn to L to face partner	Q

Regain normal hold.

15

MERENGUE

INTRODUCTION

The Merengue is the national dance of the Dominican Republic, and also to some extent, of Haiti, the neighbour sharing the island. Not only is the Merengue used on every dancing occasion in the Dominican Republic, but it is very popular throughout the Caribbean and South America, and is one of the standard Latin American dances in the USA.

There is much variety in Merengue music and most South American bands play it well. Tempos vary a great deal and the Dominicans enjoy a sharp quickening in pace towards the latter part of the dance. Normally the most favoured routine at all the clubs and restaurants that run a dance floor is a slow Bolero, breaking into a Merengue, which becomes akin to a bright, fast Jive in its closing stages. Ideally suited to the small, crowded club floors, it is a dance that is easy to learn, giving rhythmic pleasure in its movement. It seems to be gaining steadily in popularity.

THE DANCE

Music. This is written in 2/4 time; 2 beats to a bar of music, each step taking one beat. The timing in the Side Walk differs slightly and is given in the description of the figure. The tempo is 55–60 bars per minute.

Hold and Footwork. The hold is similar to the Rumba, though Merengue is sometimes danced in closer hold. The footwork is ball flat throughout.

How to learn the dance. All the figures may be preceded and followed by the Basic Side Step and may commence with the Man facing the wall and the Lady backing the wall.

The Basic Movement is typically Latin American in character, with a soft and attractive hip action that belongs to the music. Knees and hips are kept relaxed, with the shoulders steady.

The left foot is first placed to the side without weight, the knee being slightly bent, while the weight is carried on the straight right leg, with the hips pushed slightly to the right. The hips initiate the transference of weight to the left foot, moving over to the left as that leg straightens, and the right foot is brought almost to close with the left, without weight. The hips swing to the right again; weight is taken on the RF and the movement is repeated with the side step to the left. (G.W.)

Figures Described

1. *Basic Side Step*
2. *Basic Walk*
3. *Basic Side Step to Fallaway*
4. *Separation*
5. *Separation with Arm Circle*
6. *Left and Right Turns*
7. *Rhythm Movement*
8. *Promenade Flick*
9. *Windmill*
10. *The Side Walk*

1 *BASIC SIDE STEP*

Commence in Normal Hold.

	Man	Lady	Timing
	Weight on RF	Weight on LF	
1	LF to side	RF to side	1
2	RF closes, or almost closes, to LF	LF closes, or almost closes, to RF	2
3–8	Repeat 1 and 2 three times	Repeat 1 and 2 three times	1 2 1 2 1 2

May be danced with a gradual turn to the left, in a circular pattern or without turn.

2 *BASIC WALK*

Commence in Normal Hold.

	Man	Lady	Timing
	Weight on RF	Weight on LF	
1	LF forward	RF back	1
2	RF almost closes to LF	LF almost closes to RF	2
3–8	Repeat 1 and 2 three times	Repeat 1 and 2 three times	1 2 1 2 1 2

May be danced with a gradual turn to the left.

3 *BASIC SIDE STEP TO FALLAWAY*

Commence in Normal Hold.

	Man	Lady	Timing
	Weight on RF	Weight on LF	
1–4	Dance 4 steps of the Basic Side Step	Dance 4 steps of the Basic Side Step	1 2 1 2
5	LF back in Fallaway Position, turning 1/8 to left	RF back in Fallaway Position, turning 1/8 to right	1
6	Replace weight to RF in Promenade Position	Replace weight to LF in Promenade Position	2
7–8	Basic Side Step LR, turning 1/8 to right to face partner	Basic Side Step RL, turning 1/8 to left to face partner	1 2

4 *SEPARATION*

Commence in Normal Hold. Precede with the Basic Side Step.

	Man	Lady	Timing
	Weight on RF	Weight on LF	
1–8	Man and Lady place hands on partner's shoulders and take 8 small steps backwards, away from each other, hands moving down partner's arm to take a double hold		1 2 1 2
	Man—LRLRLRLR	**Lady**—RLRLRLRL	1 2 1 2
9–16	Man and Lady take 8 small steps forward, reversing the hands movement, to take normal hold		1 2 1 2
	Man—LRLRLRLR	**Lady**—RLRLRLRL	1 2 1 2

Follow with Basic Side Step or Promenade Flick.

5 *SEPARATION WITH ARM CIRCLE*

Commence in Normal Hold.

	Man	Lady	Timing
	Weight on RF	Weight on LF	
1–16	Dance the Separation. On Steps 9–12 slowly change hands to a palm-to-palm contact and on Steps 13–16 gradually raise the hands and begin to circle them outwards.		1 2 1 2 1 2 1 2
17–24	Repeat Steps 1–4 and 13–16, circling hands outwards and down and then up again to Normal Hold		1 2 1 2 1 2 1 2

Follow with Basic Side Step or Promenade Flick.

6 *LEFT AND RIGHT TURNS*

Commence in Normal Hold. Precede with Basic Side Step or Basic Side Step to Fallaway.

	Man	Lady	Timing
	Weight on RF	Weight on LF	
1	LF forward, turning to left	RF back, turning to left	1
2	RF almost closes to LF, still turning	LF almost closes to RF, still turning	2
3–6	Repeat Steps 1 and 2 twice LRLR	Repeat Steps 1 and 2 twice RLRL	1 2 1 2
7	LF back, releasing right hand, pushing Lady slightly back	RF back, releasing left hand	1
8	Replace weight to RF, taking normal hold	Replace weight to LF, taking normal hold	2
9	LF back, turning to right	RF back, turning to right	1
10	RF almost closes to LF, still turning	LF almost closes to RF, still turning	2
11–14	Repeat Steps 9 and 10 twice, LRLR	Repeat Steps 9 and 10 twice, RLRL	1 2 1 2
15	LF back in Fallaway Position	RF back in Fallaway Position	1
16	Replace weight to RF in Promenade Position. Follow with Basic Side Step	Replace weight to LF in Promenade Position turning to face partner	2

7 *RHYTHM MOVEMENT*

Commence in Normal Hold. Precede with Basic Side Step or Windmill.

	Man	Lady	Timing
	Weight on RF	Weight on LF	
1	LF to side	RF to side	1
2	RF closes to LF	LF closes to RF	2
3	Replace weight to LF, moving hips to left	Replace weight to RF, moving hips to right	1
4	Replace weight to RF, moving hips to right	Replace weight to LF, moving hips to left	2
5–8	Repeat 1–4	Repeat 1–4	1 2 1 2

Follow with Basic Walk or Windmill.

8 *PROMENADE FLICK*

Commence in Normal Hold.

	Man	Lady	Timing
	Weight on RF	Weight on LF	
1–4	Dance 4 steps of Basic Side Step LRLR	Dance 4 Steps of Basic Side Step RLRL	1 2 1 2
5	LF forward in Promenade Position, turning ¼ to left, and flick RF from the floor at back to knee level, relaxing knees	RF forward in Promenade Position, turning ¼ to right, and flick LF from the floor at back to knee level, relaxing knees	1
6	RF forward in Promenade Position	LF forward in Promenade Position	2
7–8	Dance 2 steps of Basic Side Step, LR, turning to face partner	Dance 2 steps of Basic Side Step, RL, turning to face partner	1 2

Variation of Promenade Flick:

1–4	Dance 4 steps of Basic Side Step	1 2 1 2
5–10	Dance Steps 5 and 6 three times, taking a short step on 5 and almost closing on 6	1 2 1 2 1 2

		Timing
11–12	Dance 2 steps of Basic Side Step, turning to face partner	1 2
13–16	Follow with 4 steps of Basic Side Step	1 2 1 2

9 *WINDMILL*

Commence in Normal Hold.

	Man	Lady	Timing
	Weight on RF	Weight on LF	
1–10	Precede with Steps 1–10 of Separation: on Steps 9 and 10 commence to raise arms		1 2 1 2 1 2 1 2 1 2
11–16	Both Man and Lady turn under raised arms; Man to left, Lady to right, taking 6 small steps forward for a complete turn		1 2 1 2 1 2
	Man–LRLRLR	**Lady**–RLRLRL	
17–24	Repeat the turn, taking 8 small steps forward		1 2 1 2
	Man–LRLRLRLR	**Lady**–RLRLRLRL	1 2 1 2

Finish in Normal Hold.
Follow with Basic Side Step or Rhythm Movement.

10 *THE SIDE WALK*

Commence in Normal Hold.

	Man	Lady	Timing
	Weight on RF	Weight on LF	
1–4	Dance 4 steps of the Basic Side Step	Dance 4 steps of the Basic Side Step	1 2 1 2
5	LF to side	RF to side	1
6	RF closes to LF	LF closes to RF	*and*
7–8	Repeat 5 and 6 LR	Repeat 5 and 6 RL	2 *and*
9	LF to side (long step)	RF to side (long step)	1
10	RF closes to LF	LF closes to RF	2

SUGGESTED AMALGAMATIONS

1 Basic Side Step; Basic Side Step to Fallaway; Left and Right Turns.

2 Basic Side Step; Separation; Promenade Flick; Basic Side Step.
3 Basic Side Step; Windmill; Rhythm Movement.
4 Basic Side Step; Separation with Arm Circle; Basic Side Step.
5 Basic Walk turning to Left; Separation; Basic Side Step.
6 Basic Side Step; Separation; The Side Walk.
7 Basic Side Step; Variation of Promenade Flick; Left and Right Turns.

16

MAMBO

INTRODUCTION

This dance is part of the family of Cha Cha Cha and Cuban Rumba. Its step construction is almost identical with that of the Rumba, but the music is much faster and does occasionally change its musical emphasis. When first introduced into this country the music was much too fast for most dancers and the dance did not become popular. Even now the music is rather difficult for the average dancer. However, many people travelling to exotic countries near the Equator will find this music played and will wish to have a knowledge of the dance. (P.S.)

THE DANCE

Music. Fast type of Rumba (36 bars a minute).

Footwork, Hold and Action. Because of the speed the hold is a little higher and more compact than the Rumba and Cha Cha Cha. The steps are kept small and very rhythmic, using many rock actions, almost as breathing time before the next set of steps. The action appears rather staccato, using speed to get into a figure and then the appearance of a slight pause when the figure is completed. The stance is very upright and almost regal.

Footwork is ball flat throughout, always remembering that the weight lowers late on the foot when taking a step back. The action is similar to the Rumba, but faster with less emphasis on hip action.

How to learn the dance. Practise first the six steps of the basic movement until the speed and rhythmic effect of the steps have been perfected and then gradually add one of the extra figures, practising the basic and the new figure until this is comfortable. Continue like this until one of the suggested routines has been achieved. Do not try to have a long programme of steps, you will be more successful with just a few, danced well, and will need less 'thinking' time.

Commence facing the 'outside' wall with weight on RF and work all steps from and to this position—remembering that the dance turns to the left. The alignments given are only a guide to the beginner and need not be regularly adhered to when the dancer is proficient.

Figures Described

1. *Basic*
2. *Closed Fan*
3. *New York Break and Open Rock*
4. *Shoulder to Shoulder—R and L with Alternative Basic*
5. *Cucarachas L and R*
6. *Fallaway Break*

1 *BASIC*

Commence in Closed Facing Position, Man facing wall.

	Man	Timing	Lady	Timing
1	LF forward, commencing to turn to L	2	RF back, commencing to turn to L	2
2	Replace weight to RF, continuing to turn to L	3	Replace weight to LF, continuing to turn to L	3
3	LF to side and slightly back continuing to turn to back wall	4 1	RF to side, continuing to turn to face wall	4 1
4	RF back, continuing to turn to L	2	LF forward, continuing to turn to L	2
5	Replace weight to LF, continuing to turn to L	3	Replace weight to RF, continuing to turn to L	3
6	RF to side continuing to turn to face wall	4 1	LF to side and slightly back, continuing to turn to back wall	4 1

Less turn could be made.

2 *CLOSED FAN*

Commence in Closed Facing Position, Man facing wall having danced Basic Movement.

	Man	Timing	Lady	Timing
1–3	3 steps of Basic Movement to end in Promenade Position	2 3 4 1	3 steps of Basic Movement to end in Promenade Position	2 3 4 1
4	RF back leading Lady forward outside on Man's L side, turning strongly to L	2	LF forward outside partner on Man's L side	2
5	Replace weight to LF continuing to turn	3	RF back and to side turning to L	3
6	RF to side continuing to turn to face centre	4 1	LF to side continuing to turn to back centre	4 1

End in Closed Facing Position. This figure may be repeated.

3 *NEW YORK BREAK AND OPEN ROCK*

Commence in Closed Facing Position, Man facing wall, having danced Closed Fan.

	Man	Timing	Lady	Timing
1	LF forward, small step turning to R to Counter Promenade Position	2	RF forward, small step, turning to L to Counter Promenade Position	2
2	Replace weight to RF commencing to turn L	3	Replace weight to LF commencing to turn to R	3
3	LF to side turning L to face Lady and wall	4 1	RF to side turning R to face Man and centre	4 1
4	Rock to RF in place	2	Rock to LF in place	2
5	Rock to LF in place	3	Rock to RF in place	3
6	Rock to RF in place. Type of Cucaracha with feet apart	4 1	Rock to LF with place. Type of Cucaracha with feet apart	4 1

Repeat New York Break and Open Rock. Steps 4–6 (the Open Rock) may be danced after the Fallaway Break.

4 *LEFT SHOULDER TO SHOULDER AND ALTERNATIVE BASIC MOVEMENT*

Commence in Closed Facing Position, facing diagonally to wall against LOD, weight on RF, having turned slightly to R on preceding Basic Movement ready to step outside partner on her L side.

	Man	Timing	Lady	Timing
1	LF forward outside partner on L side	2	Back RF	2
2	Replace weight to RF commencing to turn L	3	Replace weight to LF commencing to turn L	3
3	LF to side turning L to face Lady and wall	4 1	RF to side turning L to face Man and centre	4 1
4	Close RF to LF	2	Close LF to RF	2
5	Replace weight to LF	3	Replace weight to RF	3
6	Side RF preparing to step outside partner on her L side if repeating the figure	4 1	Side LF	4 1

End facing partner and wall if continuing into Basic Movement *or* diagonally to wall against LOD if repeating the figure.

RIGHT SHOULDER TO SHOULDER AND ALTERNATIVE BASIC MOVEMENT

Commence in Closed Facing Position, Man facing diagonally to wall, having danced 1–3 of Basic Movement turning slightly to L ready to step outside partner on her R side

	Man	Timing	Lady	Timing
1	RF forward outside partner on R side, facing diagonally to wall	2	Lady LF back	2
2	Replace weight to LF commencing to turn to R	3	Replace weight to RF commencing to turn to R	3

	Man	Timing	Lady	Timing
3	RF to side turning R to face Lady and wall	4 1	LF to side turning R to face Man and centre	4 1
4	Close LF to RF	2	Close RF to LF	2
5	Replace weight to RF	3	Replace weight to LF	3
6	Side LF preparing to step outside partner on her L side if repeating the R Shoulder to Shoulder *or* finish facing wall if continuing into Basic Movement	4 1	Side RF	4 1

5 *CUCARACHA MOVEMENTS*

Commence in Closed Facing Position, Man facing wall, having danced a Basic Movement, or with weight on LF, having danced 1–3 of Basic Movement or Fallaway Break

	Man	Timing	Lady	Timing
1	LF to side with part weight	2	RF to side	2
2	Replace weight to RF	3	Replace weight to LF	3
3	Close LF to RF	4 1	Close RF to LF	4 1

This movement may be danced commencing with either foot. Step 1 may be taken forward, diagonally forward, side, back or diagonally back.

6 *FALLAWAY BREAK*

Commence in Closed Facing Position, weight on RF, facing wall, having danced a Basic Movement

	Man	Timing	Lady	Timing
1	LF back in Fallaway	2	RF back in Fallaway	2
2	Replace weight to RF	3	Replace weight to LF	3
3	Close LF to RF *or* LF to side } turning R to face Lady and wall	4 1	Close RF to LF *or* RF to side } turning L to face Man and centre	4 1

Follow with Cucarachas *or* Open Rock.

SUGGESTED AMALGAMATIONS

A Basic Movement—repeated
Closed Fan repeated
and ended in Counter Promenade Position if following with:
New York and Open Rock repeated
Continue into Basic Movement

B New York Break and Open Rock repeated
Basic Movement repeated
Left Shoulder to Shoulder and
Alternative Basic repeated

C Closed Fan repeated
Fallaway Break closing on Step 3
Cucaracha Movements to R, to L
and to R
Repeat Fallaway Break stepping to
side on third step
Open Rock
Continue into Basic Movement

ORGANISATIONS WORLDWIDE

Australia: Australian Dancing Board of Control, 101 Murray Street, Perth

Federal Association of Teachers of Dancing, 161 Castlereah Street, Sydney

Austria: Verband der Tanzlehrer Osterreichs, Fleischmarkt 1, Vienna 1

Belgium: Buldo, Belgielei 46 – bus 5, 2000 Antwerpen

Canada: Canadian Dance Teachers' Association, 94 Boulevard Lavesque, Pont Viau, Laval, Quebec H7G 1C1

Ceylon: Ceylon Association of Teachers of Dancing, Kings Lynn, 2 de Forseka Road, Havelock Town, Colombo 5

China: Republic of China Council of Ballroom Dancing, P.O. Box 1780, Taipei Taiwan, China

Denmark: D.O.F., Vibevej 65, 2400 Copenhagen NV

Finland: Suomen Tanssinopettajain Liitto r.y., Voudink 6 B 35, 20780 Kaarina

France: Confederation Francaise de Maitres de Danse, 22 Rue Victor Hugo, 93110 Montreuil

Great Britain: Official Board of Ballroom Dancing, 87 Parkhurst Road, Holloway, London N7 OLP

Holland: Nederlandse Bond van Dansleraren, Toussaintkade 21, 2513 CJ Den Haag

Hong Kong: Hong Kong Dancing Association Ltd, GPO Box 6834

Iceland: Iceland Teachers of Dancing, Box 5048, Reykjavik

Indonesia: Indonesian Council of Ballroom Dancing, 29 Jln. Wolter Monginsidi, Blok Q.1. K.B. Djakarta-Selaten

Ireland: All Ireland Board of Ballroom Dancing, 7 Muckross Park, Dublin 12

Italy: FIPD, c/o Scuola di Ballo, Pietro Manazza Secretary, Via Washington 92, 20146 Milano

Associatione Nazionale Maesti di Ballo, Santa Marina 6032, Venezia 30122

Japan: Nippon Association of Teachers of Dancing, c/o The Dance and Music Ltd, Ishikawa 1st Building, Room 202, 20–1 Misakicho 2-chome, Chiyoda-ku, Tokyo (101)

Korea: The Korean Association of Ballroom Dancing, 120–3 Namyung-Dong, Yongsan-Ku, Seoul

Malaysia: Malaysian Dancers' Association, 14 Jesselton Road, Penang

New Zealand: New Zealand Council of Ballroom Dancing, 2/125 Maich Road, Manurewa, South Auckland

Norway: Norges Danselaerer-Forbund, Box 330, 5001 Bergen

Poland: Polish Dancing Society, Federacja Stowarzyszen 1, Klubow Tanecznyvh w Polsce, Kazimierza Wlk 95/5 Cracow 30-074

Scotland: Scottish Dance Teachers' Alliance, 6 Richmond Road, Bishopbriggs, Glasgow

Singapore: Singapore Ballroom Dancers Association, Room 3, 3rd Floor, Foocow Building, 21 Tyrwhitt Road, Singapore 0820

South Africa: South African Dance Teachers Association, 4 Honiball Street, Rynfield, Henoni 1500 Transvaal

Sweden: Svenges Danspedagogers Riksforbund, Box 10067, S-100 55 Stockholm

Switzerland: Swiss Official Board of Ballroom Dancing, Alpenstrasse 5, CH-6004 Lucerne

Thailand: Dance Teachers Association Thailand, 4/5 Floor, Chalemkletr Building, Krung Kaem Road, Bankok

United States: National Council of Dance Teacher Organisations, 11205 South Dixie Highway, Suite 200, Miami, Florida 33156

West Germany: Allgemeiner Deutscher Tanzlehrer Verband Jacobistrasse 18, 4000 Dusseldorf

Yugoslavia: Slovene Dancing Teachers' Association 61111 Ljubljana P.P. 33